Benjamin Franklin Leggett

A Sheaf of Song

Benjamin Franklin Leggett

A Sheaf of Song

ISBN/EAN: 9783744770446

Printed in Europe, USA, Canada, Australia, Japan

Cover: Foto ©Thomas Meinert / pixelio.de

More available books at **www.hansebooks.com**

A SHEAF OF SONG.

BY

BENJ. F. LEGGETT.

AUTHOR OF "A TRAMP THROUGH SWITZERLAND."

Taketh the fruyt and let the chaf be stille.—CHAUCER.

NEW YORK:
JOHN. B. ALDEN, PUBLISHER.
1887.

TO MY MOTHER

THESE GLEANINGS FROM THE

HARVEST FIELDS OF MANY YEARS

ARE AFFECTIONATELY

DEDICATED.

CONTENTS.

	PAGE.
The Ballad of the King	7
Capri	13
Burns' Birthday	15
The Comet	18
Eventide	19
Threescore	19
A Morning Song	21
Possession	22
Castle Windows	22
Beyond	24
Outward Bound	25
On the Heights	26
Alpine Echoes	27
A Word for Shakespeare	28
Anniversary	30
Our Baby	31
An Autumn Idyl	32
Ruins	33
Another Year	36
Consider the Lilies	36
In Camp	37
December	39
To J. E	40
An Ancestral Ode	41
On a Fir-cone from Bayard Taylor's Grave	44
Indian Summer	45
An Old Story Retold	46
Old and New	48
In Springtime	49
Peter Cooper	50
The Children's Day	51

CONTENTS.

	PAGE.
On Reading an Old Poet	55
To E. A. B	56
October	56
Mt. McGregor—July 23, 1885	59
A Song in the Night	59
Sugar Time	61
At Last	61
Chippewanoxetti	63
Birthday	63
Nature's Plan	64
To H. W. Longfellow	65
On Pilgrimage	66
At Cedarcroft	66
To my Mother on her Birthday	68
Only Four	70
June	71
In War-time—1864	73
To G. G. B	74
Lake Albano	74
An Alpine Lake	75
In the Hammock	76
On a Fossil Shell	77
The First Decade	78
In the Soudan	80
Orion	82
Ponte St. Angelo	82
Round Lake	83
Thanksgiving—1866	86
Keats' Grave	87
To Oliver Wendell Holmes	88
Ravenswood	88
My Inheritance	91
Christmas	93
In Peace	95
At Dawn	95
April Days	96
Some After-Supper Lines	97
At the Gate	100
To John G. Whittier	101
Our Refuge	102

	PAGE.
Enfranchised	103
Only Two Summers	104
Under the Willows	106
After the War	108
Day by Day	111
The New Succession	111
Trust	112
The New Year	113
King Midas	114
My Quest	117
A Battle Relic	118
The Herb Called Heart's-Ease	120
On the Hills	121
To H. W. Longfellow on His Birthday	122
"Watchman! What of the Night?"	124
Passing the Light	126
For the Brave	126
For a Crystal Wedding	127
Decoration Day	130
A New Year's Greeting—To J. G. W.	131
To a Dead Poet	132
Dickens in Westminster Abbey	133
Lines read on the Tenth Anniversary of St. John's Literary Association, Sept. 17, 1885	134
The Dying Year	145
Gladstone	146
To a Nonagenarian	146
For a Silver Wedding	147
Morning	148
Absence	149
A Summer Madrigal	150
The Age of Gold	151

A SHEAF OF POEMS.

THE BALLAD OF THE KING.

What dawns would light the world again,
  What shadows flee away,
What angels walk once more with men
  If only Love held sway!

An olden story:—ponder well
  This legend here re-told,
How love dissolved a wicked spell
  In knightly days of old.

'Twas in the age of old renown—
  Long since the years have flown,
But still their glory fading down
  Regilds with light our own.

Then Arthur ruled with gentle sway
  And woke the minstrel song,
And mail-clad men in grand array,
  Went forth against the wrong.

No baffled cause might vainly plead
  For aid in knightly ear,

For Arthur's self gave royal heed
   To beauty's smile and tear.

'Twas while he bravely fought and well
   For maid in castle wall,
That he, through dire enchantment's spell,
   Became a lowly thrall.

Now in brave Arthur's fallen state
   The king shone true and grand,
As when with his retainers late.
   He rode through all the land.

The wizard marked his royal grace
   And signed that they should bring
His lowly captive face to face
   With him, the mighty king!

"Vain man! go forth beneath my spell
   A twelvemonth and a day,
If then your wisdom answers well
   My question—go your way.

"But if the tale is then untold
   What women one and all,
Do more desire than fame, or gold,
   Ye still shall be my thrall."

Then with the sun the king rode forth
   And wandered east and west,
Through sunny south and frozen north
   Upon his royal quest.

And while he roamed the summer passed,
   And autumn tints of flame,

Burned low to ashen gray at last,
  And still no answer came.

The winter fled and spring grew gay
  With violets hidden long;
That bloomed beside his weary way,
  And earth was glad with song.

All vainly seemed the quest to grow
  Till once he drew his rein,
At sight of one so foul and low,
  He spurned her with disdain.

"O captive king, whose blinded zeal
  Doth spurn my low degree,
Perchance thy quest I may reveal,
  Though foul I am to see."

"If this thou canst,"—his heart was stirred—
  While nearer still he came—
"Then thou shalt have, I pledge my word,
  Whatever ye may claim."

"Then swear me this:—Of those who throng
  Your royal court so wide,
Some brave young knight, both fair and strong,
  Shall wed me for his bride!"

She took this pledge of matchless worth,
  Then did her own fulfill:—
"What woman values more than earth
  Is but her own sweet will!"

Then light of heart King Arthur sought
  Through cool, sweet forest shade,

The wizard's home, and answer brought
   The loathsome hag had made.

And lo! the spell so strong before
   Could not the truth gainsay—
The charm was broken, and once more
   The king went on his way.

Then straight unto his palace wall
   He rode all free and grand,
No more enchantment's lowly thrall,
   But ruler of the land!

Now when for valliant knight and lord
   A royal feast was laid,
The king rehearsed to all the board
   The pledge which he had made.

And when he asked of all the band
   Who forth the hag would bring,
And place upon her withered hand
   The golden wedding-ring?

Fair knights who fain would bravely dare
   All foes in beauty's name,
All hung their heads in silence there
   Beneath the flush of shame.

Now of King Arthur's royal band
   Who drew the knightly rein
None truer was in all the land
   Than fair and brave Gewain!

The youngest knight was he of all,
   And proudly flashed his eye,

When to his sovereign's royal call
  None older made reply.

" No royal pledge shall be denied!
  Bring forth the golden ring :—
The loathsome hag shall be my bride
  For honor of the king!"

And 'mid the summer's passing state
  He clasped the withered hand,
Of her who in her mean estate
  Was lowest of the land!

And so the loathsome and the fair
  Before the king were wed—
By knight and hag in solemn prayer
  The marriage vows were said.

But 'ere the royal feast had rest,
  From all the menial train,
Gewain had heard the whispered jest
  That filled his heart with pain.

And when the festal hours were flown,—
  The bridal chamber nigh,
So sad of heart the knight had grown
  He only longed to die!

But when he sought his rest at last
  With weary sigh and moan,
Before his gaze such beauty passed
  As he had never known!

No more in hated hideousness
  Did she before him stand,

But clothed in queenliest loveliness!—
   The beauty of the land!

Then did the bride to him confess
   The secret kept so well,
How all her hated loathsomeness
   Was but the wizard's spell!

And since the bridal-ring she wore
   The charm was half o'er-thrown—
Now half the time that form she bore
   And half the time her own!

Now would he choose that she should wear
   Her beauty's sweet array,
By night when none would know her fair
   Or in the light of day?

But when he thought a moment's space
   Of bitter jest and scorn,
Her beauty in its matchless grace,
   He fain would keep for morn!

Then breathing love's divinest stress
   She told in tender tone,
How all her fairest loveliness
   Was but for him alone!

Then with the grace that beauty lent
   The tenderest heart to thrill,
The gentle knight gave love's consent
   To beauty's own sweet will!

And then the charm was *wholly* flown
   By night and day as well,—

The love that made his will her own
    Dissolved the wizard's spell.

Then henceforth queen of beauty grand
    In Arthur's royal train,
None fairer lived in all the land
    Than bride of brave Gewain!—

And still whatever spell may harm,
    What influence grasp and hold,
Love still retains the potent charm
    It held in days of old!

O rosy dawn, light up again
    The glad unclouded day,
When angels here shall walk with men
    And only Love hold sway!

CAPRI.

O BLOOD-RED jasper from the haunted bay
    Whose blue waves fondled thee,
I marvel that thou wearest not to-day
    The azure of the sea.

Hast thou no dream within thy warm heart kept
    Of tender skies bent low?
Of waves that sang while white foam softly crept
    To touch thy lips with snow?

I gaze on thee; dream-like my eyelids close
    While far sweet glories smile;
No more I see the drifted winter snows,
    But Capri's wave-beat isle.

The splintered crown of some lone mountain range
   Uplifted bold and free,
With dizzy crags of beauty wild and strange
   That hang above the sea,

Alone she stands, arrayed in purple hue
   And fringed with foam and spray,
Her rifted slopes still mirrored in the blue,
   And sphered by sky and bay.

Again her paths are trod by eager feet
   Slow toiling from below,
And from her groves of lemon, cool and sweet
   The airs of summer blow.

From time-worn crags that watch the beaten shore,
   And landward look and lean,
St. Elmo's towers, above the azure floor,
   And Ischia's heights are seen.

And like the incense of an offered prayer
   Or smoke of sacrifice,
The dread volcano's white breath climbs the air
   And mounts the summer skies.

A dreamy sound of voices from below
   Floats up along the breeze,
And like the sea-birds ever come and go
   The ships from Indian seas.

I seem to hear the lisp of dreaming palms
   From lone Sahara's rim,
As south winds bring between the pulseless calms
   The desert's wandering hymn.

All sounds and voices and the mellow light
   Of that far sunny land,
Fade out at last before the stormy night
   That beats our Northern strand.

O blood-red jasper! warm with sunset glow
   Caught from the wave and sky,
Thou holdest still above the frost and snow
   The dreams that never die.

BURNS' BIRTHDAY.

O ROYAL-HEARTED Robert Burns,
   So tender, true and strong!
We crown again his natal day
   With rustic wreath of song.

In every land, or near or far,
   His gentle name is known;
His songs far sweeping round the world
   On wings of fame have flown.

Through all the dim-aisled century
   His living numbers swell,
For well the poet wrought his charm
   And wove his magic spell.

To-day his words are sweeter still
   On music's trembling tongue,
And all the world is greener far
   Since he has lived and sung.

While on his hills the gray light dawns,
   The songful day returns,

We tread again the bonnie land
   So loved by Robert Burns!

What charm lies on her purple heights,
   And on her meadows fair,
As in a dream we wander forth
   A sweet June day in Ayr.

The flowing waters through the town
   The gray old arches lave,
And Wallace's tower stands stark and still
   To hear the Twa Brigs rave.

There stands O'Shanter's cozy inn
   A refuge from the storm,
Where Tam so gloriously forgot
   The wrath at home so warm!

'Mid meadow lands of clover bloom
   And clumps of snowy thorn,
Beneath the lowly thatch we stand
   Where baby Burns was born!

Glad bird-songs with the sunshine come
   To cheer the dusky gloom,
As though the old sweet lullaby
   Yet lingered in the room.

Beyond is auld Kirk Alloway,
   All roofless save the sky,
Where witch-fires lighted up the dark
   As Tam rode reeling by.

Ah, how the warlock revel rang,
   And how the windows glowed,

BURNS' BIRTHDAY.

Tam by all the clan pursued
Went thundering down the road!

Oh, what a goblin ride was that,
    To make the stoutest quail,
In sooth it saved the man his life,
    But cost gray Meg her tail!

The Auld Brig clasps the banks of Doon,
    The river slides away,
The hoof-beats of that hurried flight
    Will ring and sound for aye.

The bonnie braes of Doon are glad
    Through winding curves and turns,
And birds repeat by burn and mere
    The name of Robin Burns!

No daisies bloom beside the way,
    Nor star with pearl and gold
The broad green belt of meadow-lands,
    But still his memory hold.

His birthday 'mid the Scottish hills
    Is glad with love and song,
For dear they hold his precious name,
    And burning hate of wrong:

For high above the shams of rank,
    Or accident of birth,
He set the royalty of man
    And loved him for his worth.

So comes the poet's natal day
    With joy and gladness in :—

For him the pure sweet charity
    Which covers every sin.

Be just: speak not of wasted years,
    But let his virtues shine;—
Above his weak humanity
    Was faith in the Divine!

THE COMET.

Far alone through the chartless seas she came,
    Where never a sail was unfurled,
Till she shook the reefs from her folded flame
    For a cruise by many a world!

Through the measureless years, her red lights shone
    On the nebulous whirlpool spray—
On the trackless surf of the stars far blown
    And the foam of the milky-way!

And the drifting worlds caught her flaming light
    And her banner above unrolled,
As she plowed her way with a tireless might
    Round the cape of the sun's red gold.

How grandly she swept!—how her head-lights burned!
    At the sunward dip of her spars,
With the joy of the outward-bound she turn
    Flag-ship of the fleet of the stars!

Speed ever and on, O craft of the skies!
    Afar through the infinite spheres,

Past the utmost seas where the world-waves
    rise,
  On thy cruise of the untold years.

EVENTIDE.

The ghostly heat of summer noon is laid,
  The pallid fever of his reign is spent;
A world-wide blessing woven of the shade,
  Cool evening lifts the star-folds of her tent.

A subtle hint of balm is in the air:
  The breath of flowers in dream-enfolded sleep
Floats like the incense of a lifted prayer,
  While insect murmurs rhythmic measure, keep.

The valley's dusk in dewy silence lies,
  For labor's song and weary tumult cease:
The stars in quiet hold the summer skies,
  And evening wears her perfect crown of peace.

THREESCORE.

The white day comes again, dear wife,
  In beauty's flush and glow,
As first upon our wedded life
  It dawned so long ago:—
That golden morn whose sweet light lay
  On plighted hearts and hands,
Far kindling into rosy day
  The yet untrodden lands.

Though fair the beckoning years before
  To love-lit vision seemed,

How well we know their golden store
    Was vaster than we dreamed:
For through the vanished summer, flown
    Our footsteps all the while
Have bloomed with joys which love has grown
    Beneath her patient smile.

With backward look we pass to-day,
    Two pilgrims further bound,
Another mile-stone on lifes way
    With autumn roses crowned.
And viewing all the past again,
    Its hoarded wealth untold,
We know the years that yet remain
    Hold love's uncounted gold.

Beyond us rise the height sublime,
    And nearer, hill on hill,
The rosy smile of morning-time,
    In vision lingers still.
While speed the swiftly changing scenes
    Across our pilgrim way,
Still o'er our path a glory leans
    That gladdens every day.

So tread we on with patient feet
    The winding pathway through,
While two hearts hold for aye complete.
    The old love always new.
Though summer-time may lose its crown
    The dry leaves lisp and fall,
Across the slope we journey down,
    And love is all in all.

A MORNING SONG.

O FAIR and sweet is the summer morn—
    A queen in her beauty crowned—
A mist-wreath over her shoulders flung
    With pearls and diamonds bound.

So softly over the hills she came,
    As still as the roses blow,
The valleys asleep heard not her step,
    But woke at her smile aglow.

Her presence wore such a queenly grace
    That the shadows gave her room,
She sweetened the air with dewy breath,
    And kissed the flowers a-bloom.

So the clover-heads, and the buttercups,
    And the daisies' white-rayed gold,
With the royal lilies sweet and tall
    Her treasure and blessing hold.

The meadows swept by her garments' hem
    Are beaded with gems of dew,
And the maple leaves for joy of her
    Are tremulous through and through.

O brooding peace of the morning, stay!
    Nor swift as her presence fly,
Sing aye, my heart, as the wild birds sing,
    While the sweet morn passes by.

POSSESSION.

On wildwood slopes where April lays
    Her wooing touch so tender,
To break the sleep of winter days
    And waken starry splendor,
The Mayflower hides her modest worth
    From gaze of curious seeing,
But still betrays her blissful birth
    By odorous joy of being.

Deep in the dusk of tangled dells,
    Else full of gloom and sadness,
The thrush's song of beauty swells
    In sweet unmeasured gladness:
No ear may note the tender strain
    The songful heart is giving,
Still on it flows in sweet refrain—
    The very bliss of living.

The starriest splendor shuns the day
    Nor wears its crown unbidden,—
The rarest beauty hides away,
    The sweetest songs are hidden:—
The poet's brow may wear the bays,
    His name be ever ringing,
But still above the sweetest praise
    He holds the joy of singing.

CASTLE WINDOWS.

From my spacious castle windows—
    Airy castles of the brain—
I have looked abroad and listened,
    Heard the bugle's mellow strain,

Seen the pageant's passing splendor
   With its glories manifold,
Seen the cloud-built towers illumined
   With the dying sunset's gold,
And the dawn's far-reaching banners
   From their pinnacles unrolled.

Full before the open casement
   Fairest visions sweep and throng,
While the castle arches tremble
   With the melody of song.
Gleams of eastern lands of story,
   Fairy realms of old renown,
Crumbling walls whose faded glory
   Wears the ivy's leafy crown,
While above the Neckar valley
   Far and wide the ruins frown.

Tower and bastion rise below me,
   On the mountain slope I stand,
And the vision waits before me
   Of the glorious Fatherland.
From the forest wilds of Odin
   Sweeps the river to the plain,
Where the castled Rhine rolls onward
   To the breakers of the main,
And the meadow-lands are golden
   With the largess of the rains.

Where the vineyard slopes are purple
   With the vintage of the year,
Rings the mellow voice of labor
   And the harvest songs of cheer:
Down the mountains paths I wander
   To the ruins old and brown,

Where the riven towers uplifted
   Watch above the quaint old town,
By the storied river dreaming,
   With the castle for its crown.

Over castle, hill and mountain,
   Still the autumn sunsets burn,
And the olden days long vanished
   From the dusky past return:
Still the airy windows kindle
   With a changeful glow and gleam,
Like the hues of fairy splendor
   From the jewel's prisoned beam;
And the vision passes onward
   Like the glory of a dream.

BEYOND.

Where stays the year which waits to bring
   Our long and last repose,
Whose golden gates shall open swing
   For us, but never close?

What fair, sweet month of all the year
   Shall pillow on her breast
Our weariness, and drop her tear
   Above our dreamless rest?

When will the day so far and wide
   In dawn's fair beauty bloom,
Whose flowers will stand for us aside
   And yield a little room?

Just where the final mile-stone stands,
   Or where the meadows end,

Whose fringes touch the unknown lands,
    And with the twilight blend,

Our blindness cannot see, or know,
    Amid the dim earth-shine,
Yet Heaven's immortal lilies blow
    But just across the line.

And sometime on that border land,
    Beyond the last, long mile,
We'll clasp again the vanished hand
    And greet the olden smile.

OUTWARD BOUND.

Out of the misty blue of the West
    We sweep with our sails unfurled,
Out of the West and into the East,
    Away with the rolling world.

Across the heaving disc of the sea,
    Enzoned with a ring of mist,
Our reeling track is white with the foam
    And fringed with the amethyst.

Above the horizon's glowing rim
    Dawn's fiery splendor crawls,
And the mid-day sun rolls down the steep,
    And into the ocean falls.

Across the sweep of the star-hung blue
    The Zodiac's monsters shine,
And gloss themselves in the starry wave,
    Then drop in the azure brine.

Afar through the gray and ghostly mist—
   The pallid and boding gloom
Whose fringes are torn by tempest wings
   And the fog-horn's dismal boom—

Away and away, our foaming track
   Reels ever from strand to strand,
Till the crags of the Old World lifted high
   With a welcome, give us land!

ON THE HEIGHTS.

Where dizzy ledges cleave the upper blue
   And stunted balsams grow,
I breathe the freedom of the hills anew
   And pause to look below.

So far beneath the winding valley lies,
   No sound from thence can come
To scale the crags uplifted to the skies—
   All life below is dumb.

Around the space wherein the valley winds,
   As if to guard and bless,
Throng crowded leagues of ever-murmuring pines,
   A swarthy wilderness.

Across the meadows drift the shadows fleet,
   From island mists air-blown,
Whose trailing fringes are beneath my feet
   Upon this mountain throne.

Beyond the hills, across the wooded land,
   The storm-winged legions go;

The sunshine falls around me where I stand
   The thunder rolls below.

And pausing here upon the heights sublime
   To rest on beds of fern,
Afar I see from crags of eldest time
   The clouds all golden burn.

Beneath me moans the tempest's angry pain;
   While livid lightnings play,
His stormy passion crumbles into rain,
   And weeps itself away.

Upon the heights where peace and sunshine sleep,
   And heaven is always blue,
Dwell thou, O pilgrim, and forever kee
   Life's sunward side in view.

ALPINE ECHOES.

Fair valley stream, so glad with mellow song,
   And low, sweet laughter's gurgling melody,
   Whose crystal feet are tripping toward the s
Thy voice I hear as when the idle throng
Of golden days in fair procession long
   Hung tranced above thy beauty's dimpled grace,
   And white and cool across the far blue space
The snowy cones were lifted clear and strong!
And far above the tinkling bells I hear
   From snow-fringed pastures, green with summer's crown,
And mountain songs are ringing sweet and clear
   From lifted slopes of sunshine drifting down.—
O far-off voices of the vanished days,
Whose echoes linger and whose sweetness stays!

A WORD FOR SHAKESPEARE.

When hawthorn hedges, foaming white,
    Were sweet with mimic snowing,
He first beheld the April light
    And heard the Avon flowing.

Like other children, then as now,
    The olden summers found him,
He laughed and cried and knit his brow,
    And ruled the world around him!

Still was he wiser than they knew—
    This child, the straw-thatch under,
Whose song three hundred years ago
    Yet makes the wide world wonder!

A child, from croon of cradle hymn
    Above him in his slumbers,—
A youth, along the Avon's rim
    He caught his tuneful numbers.

Full poet-souled the shy boy grew
    To manhood's ripe completeness;
What Nature taught he quickly knew—
    Her wondrous lore and sweetness.

The years so fraught with weary toil
    Were gladdened by his singing,
For well he heard through life's turmoil
    Serenest music ringing:

As everywhere the world-wide throng
    To-day who know and love him,

Through his can hear the lark's sweet song,
   That soared and sang above him.

Where'er he turned his eager feet,
   Her smile o'er him was leaning,
He felt the heart of Nature beat,
   And learned its hidden meaning.

What golden wealth from her he brought—
   Her heir by this sweet token—
A power to clothe the hidden thought
   That else had been unspoken.

What marvel that the race to-day
   Toward him is fondly turning,
Who gave its hope a tongue for aye
   To tell its deathless yearning?

All changing moods of being's state,
   Life's sad or sunny fancies,
The smile of love, the scowl of hate,
   Affection's sweet romances,

He holds embalmed in wondrous art—
   A lore beyond the sages—
The wildest passions of the heart,
   The tenderest love-lit pages.

Grand builder in the realm of thought!
   Through his wide-swinging portals,
Behold the fane his fancy wrought,
   And peopled with immortals!

The king of bards he stands revealed,
   By very grace of giving,—

What hidden founts hath he unsealed,
   And poured for all the living!

His fame and song ring evermore
   Above the centuries' thunders;—
Though dead three hundred years and more,
   Yet still the wide world wonders!

ANNIVERSARY.

Dear wife, behold our wedding day!
   How swift the years have flown—
A score of summers ebbed away
   Since you became my own!

This glad sweet morn of summer's prime,
   Whose dawn but just appears,
Fills up and rounds the measured time
   Of twenty wedded years!

What fairer dawns of splender rare
   Have set our hills aglow,
Far grander than the vision fair
   Of twenty years ago!

And life yet wears the perfect crown
   That never groweth old;—
Love faileth not but ripens down
   With autumn's ruddy gold.

And now, dear wife, while sunset gleams
   Across our valleys play,
The choice of boyhood's glowing dreams
   Is manhood's choice to-day!

OUR BABY.

Have you seen our baby?
    Wait a moment—stay,
Here she is—our treasure,
    Two months old to-day!

Have you seen her equal
    Ever?—anywhere?
Note her blue eyes tender,
    And her silken hair!

See her soft cheeks dimpled
    By the smiles that play—
Cheeks like tinted blossoms
    Of the peach in May.

Lips like berries ripened
    In the summer days,
This is sober earnest—
    Can I *over*-praise?

See her fingers clasping,
    See her hands outreach,
Hear the cooing music
    Of her baby speech.

With the next sweet summer
    When she comes to words,
Won't she rival fairly
    All the singing birds?

When she came she brought us
    Bliss without alloy—

Mother's blessed darling,
    Father's perfect joy.

Fairest petalled blossom
    On life's spreading tree,—
Little Princess Royal,
    Queen of hearts is she!

None-such she is truly,
    Doubt it if you can.
Could a world of treasure
    Buy our Baby Fan?

Have *you* got a baby?
    Nay?—It's very sad!
Honestly and truly
    Don't you wish you had?

AN AUTUMN IDYL.

The autumn sunset burning low
    Floods all the silent air,
The frosted maples wear a glow
    Like saintly nuns at prayer.

Upon the uplands growing brown
    Flames yet the golden-rod,
And silently the thistle-down
    Is sowing all the sod.

The forest robes upon the hills
    The breezes lift and blow,
Baring the beauty of the rills,
    White-breasted as the snow.

Across the lands all richly dight
    A royal pageant strays,
With crimson banners bathed in light,
    And russet gold ablaze.

With queenly grace the year goes down
    The sunset slopes the while,
Upon her head October's crown
    And on her face a smile.

RUINS.

I.

By the woods and meadow-lands
Still the leaning ruin stands;
Old and mossy, stained and gray,
Slowly crumbling to decay.
Rank weeds round the hearth-stone grow,
Where the red coals used to glow
In the winters long ago.
Through rent roof and rifted walls
Blue sky gleams and sunshine falls,
Autumn's rain and winter's snow
And birds of summer come and go:
Come, and on the rafters brown,
Under broad eaves sloping down,
In the braces, on the stays,
In the chimney's crooked ways
Build their nests and linger long
Till the blue eggs turn to song,
And the gables out of reach
Are musical with tender speech.

II.

Thus we find it filled with song
After years of absence long,
And the notes of many birds
Seem the echoes of the words
Childhood's voices sweet and low
Uttered in the long ago.
How the vanished past appears
Through the mist of faded years!
Musing 'mid these dreamy sounds
Glimpse we vales whose sacred grounds
We shall never, soon nor late,
Tread again, nor pass the gate.
Though the doors swing open wide
Only outward footsteps glide:—
Dreaming only may we stand
Within the gates of childhood's land.

III.

Backward through the golden haze
Look we on the olden days.
Fair the sunshine trembled through
The freshness of the morning dew—
Morn that broadened all too soon
Into fervid heats of noon.
Never bluer skies outspread
Tent-like over childish head;—
Never wild birds sang more sweet—
   Potent charm to stay our feet—
Wildwood blossoms swinging wide
Seemed to beckon us aside:
Song of bird or nod of flower
Gave us many a truant hour,

When through shadows sweet and cool
We took the wood-path way to school.

IV.

Many, many years have fled,—
Some are living, many dead
Who within the pine's thick shade
In the golden summers played.
From the hillside sloping down,
Where the greenwood waved its crown,
And the shadows of the pines
Formed and marched in spectral lines,
Tramping with their silent feet
Out through clover blossoms sweet,—
Waving dusky hands of gloom
Through the meadow's fringe of bloom,—
All have vanished, all have flown
Save where one tree makes its moan
And the ruin stands alone.

V.

When the wide-mouthed chimney high,
Upward staring at the sky,
Holds no more the mellow note
Of nested swallows in its throat,—
When the memory-haunted wall,
Roof and rafter lean and fall,
And the passing years efface
Every vestige of its place,
We shall feel with throbs of pain
Something lost beyond regain.

ANOTHER YEAR.

Another year, and still another year,
   And yet no fruit is found;
The bloom has faded and the leaves are sere,
   Why cumbereth it the ground?

The dews of heaven distil upon it there—
   Of sun and rain no lack;
It takes all bounty from the earth and air
   And renders nothing back.

No golden fruit—a richly measured meed
   Of praise for bounties strown :—
A feeble type of our ungrateful greed
   The fig-tree stands alone.

Another year of sleepless care may bring
   The long delayed return,
And birds of praise may in the branches sing,
   And ripe fruits hang and burn.

Another year, dear Lord, another year
   Spare thou as in the past,—
The later blooms may hang mid leaves all sere
   Some golden fruit at last.

CONSIDER THE LILIES.

Out of the dust the lilies spring,
   Up from the blackest mould,
Touched by the sunbeam's flaming wing
   They stand in pearl and gold.

Never a king on his gilded throne
   Arrayed in jewels rare,

With half the princely glory shone
   The royal lilies wear.

Out of the dust their beauty gleams
   Only a summer's day,
Mocking the pride of human dreams
   With royalest array:

Nor toil, nor spin for robes they wear,—
   Under His hand they grow,
Beyond all beauty of compare
   And only bloom and blow.

Why take ye thought:—the Master's word—
   For robes that fade and fall?
Alike he cares for flower and bird,
   Are ye not more than all?

More than the lilies' royal worth,
   More than her robes of gold,
The endless years of another birth
   After our dream is told.

Out of the dust and of the dust,
   Akin to the soulless clod,
We climb by the rounds of faith and trust
   To the endless life of God!

IN CAMP.

A HUNTER's camp by forest lake
   With many a range around,
Of fir-fringed slopes and purple peaks,—
   A wild enchanted ground.

High over all the twilight heaven,
    Below the waves at rest,
The green gems of the wooded isles
    Asleep on beauty's breast.

The blue smoke of the camp-fire curls
    In waved and twisted lines,
Across the trembling aspen leaves,
    Among the whispering pines.

Sweet nature's hush is in the air,
    And on the water lies,
Whose crystal deeps give back the blush
    Of evening's tender skies.

White mists are floating on the hills;
    Across the silent air
Broad arms are spread in blessing forth
    To make the scene more fair.

Against the blue-walled firmament
    The curved and airy bars
Of vapor gleam like sabre blades
    With jewelled hilts of stars.

In ashen white the camp-fire veils
    Its faint and pallid gleams,
While on the odorous balsam boughs
    We pass to quiet dreams.

Till touched by midnight's magic spell,
    From starriest dreams we wake,
To see the soft light on the hills,
    The white mist on the lake

Fold silently pale spectral arms
   Across its jewelled breast—
The naiad of the waters set
   To guard its starry rest.

And thus while on the barren hills
   The drifted snows are piled
By winter gales exultingly,
   With voices fierce and wild,

The summer camp in wildwood glades,
   The forest's shaded ways,
Pass in review and charm again
   As in the golden days.

Hang ever thus, O forest scenes,
   Amid the starry throng
Of hours that mock the fairest dreams,
   That shame the sweetest song.

DECEMBER.

O MONTH of song and wail!
   O month of mirth and cheer!
With voice of storm and gale
   Sing out the waning year.

Sing to the woodlands bare,
   Sing to the hillsides brown,
Drop from the misty air
   Thy snowy mantle down.

Hang where the wood-slope grieves
   For robes of summer lost,

Pearls for the faded leaves,
   And beaded stars of frost.

O lull with frost and frown
   The streamlets' noisy flow,
To mellow chime from fairy town,
   Under the drifted snow.

Weave thou for waiting lands
   Rare robes with ermine frills,
And fold them with thy jeweled hands
   Around the shivering hills.

Breathe with thy frosty breath,
   And paint on window-pane,
Mosses and ferns and heath,
   And lilies wet with rain,

Grasses and leaves and sprays,
   Forests and fanes and spires,
And mountain peaks ablaze
   With light of opal fires.

And thus, O month of storms!
   Give for the flowers that blow,
Old winter's mythic forms
   Of bloom in frost and snow.

TO J. E.

O weary friend! to whom has come at last
   The blissful rest, the calm and perfect peace,
   And full fruition after toils release,—
I give thee joy for all the victories past!

This wreath of song upon thy grave I cast:
  Could thy fond ear but catch the simple strain,
  Then wouldst thou know how through all grief
    and pain
Love lingers yet, while tears fall thick and fast.
  Through fitful starlight crossed with banded gloom
To dawn's white splendor have thy feet attained;—
  The hills whereon immortal lilies bloom
Are thine, aye,—the goal forever gained!
And so we part, till from the star-lit skies
On us who wait the unclouded dawn shall rise:
1881.

AN ANCESTRAL ODE.

Why toil in rhyme? Dull, common prose
Could never half my thought disclose;
And e'en the stately tread of rhyme
Perchance may fail the theme sublime.
Yet Atlas, toiling 'neath his load
Along the hot and dusty road,
With brawny shoulders bent and bare
Beneath his ponderous world of care,
Might smooth his wrinkled brow and smile
To trade his pack for mine awhile.

Shall I essay the utmost rim
Where distant suns burn pale and dim;
Or seek the hidden cause to know
Which makes our burning sunsets glow
With crimson splendor soft and clear
Through earth's transfigured atmosphere?
Nay, but I leap the mighty chasm

Beyond the reach of protoplasm,
And sail, and sail, the shoreless sea
Of matter's mighty protency!
Ah! theme sublime! who shall aspire
To any bolder flight, or higher?

Since longing will supply the wing
And teach the humble bat to sing,
Then why may we not mount and fly
As song-birds through the summer sky?
How frail the walls which hold us in
Since we are all one kith and kin
With earth's wide fauna! What a dream!—
Surpassing strange this wondrous theme!

How passing sweet to linger here,—
To trace our growth from sphere to sphere,
To that far mystic time and age—
The morning of our pilgrimage,
As evolution strangely tells,
When we were mollusks in our shells!
Doubt not: the crisp, sweet oyster pie
Is luscious by a kindred tie!

But ages ere the bivalve grew
What vast development he knew!
From primal matter's potent strife
Dead atoms took the cue of life,
Because they must, and might, and should,
And could'nt help it if they would!
And then the molecules by dozens—
Our ancient, dear ancestral cousins—
Swarmed out like bees from summer hive
And made the universe alive!—

So Darwin says, though some still scout it,
But Huxley 'll tell you all about it.

Was it, in sooth, a silly whim
In hoary æons old and dim,
That discontented bivalves yearned
Till they to wriggling tadpoles turned?
Not so; progressions never fail—
Each bivalve gained thereby a tail!
And wrestling with a dumb desire,
He still aspired to something higher,
Till changed again, as we may see,
At last a leaping frog was he,
Rejoicing in his liberty!

And now what hasty strides he made!
Development, so long delayed,
Moved on apace, as well it should,
From kangaroo to monkeyhood:
Orang-outang and chimpanzee
Are in his line of ancestry;
Till from progression's mighty span
Emerged the stately creature—man!
All hail, illustrious pedigree!
We bow and own our ancestry!
What upright forms of graceful shape
Developed from the grinning ape!
What brain and brawn, a priceless boon,
Transmitted from the sage baboon!
Where lives the man whose very spine,
At thought of his ancestral line,
Has not been thrilled with filial pride
Till he for very joy has cried?

If such there be, go mark him well,
For him no minstrel measures swell "
From blithsome fen, or reedy pool,
Where kindred hold their singing-school.
Their alto, bass and baritone
No witching spell o'er him have thrown;
He hears no song from shore to shore,
And so he bars and bolts his door,
Forgetful of the starry shine
That crowns his long ancestral line!

ON A FIR CONE FROM BAYARD TAYLOR'S GRAVE.

TO J. G. W.

When last the autumn's changeful glory gave
  To field and woodland all its splendor rare,
  While dreamful beauty melted through the air,
This fragrant cone dropped on the poet's grave.
And now while storms of winter wildly rave,
  I hear again the rhythm sweet and strong
  That trembled through the fir-tree's solemn song
As in its shade I saw its branches wave.
And still it sings of weary journeys done,
  Of northern pines and drooping tropic palms,
Of desert sands and snowy summits won,
  Of mingled storms and sunshine and of calms,
And welcome home!—a lullaby that thrills
The listening silence of his native hills!

INDIAN SUMMER.

When spring-time sun and tender rain
   Had set the buds aflame,
The royal gates swung wide again
   And queenly Summer came.

Fair maiden queen of all the year—
   God's beauty in the land,
We greeted her with smile and cheer,
   We clasped her jewelled hand.

Through quiet haunts and dreamy dells
   We went where wood-birds build,
In meadow vales, on upland swells,
   Where sweetest songs are trilled.

In queenly ways of loveliness,
   'Mid all things fair and sweet,
And fondly did the glad earth press
   Her flower-ensandaled feet.

Through golden days we wandered wide—
   She led through sun and shade,
And all the land seemed glorified
   Where'er her footsteps strayed.

Where wild-birds sang on wooded heights
   And laughed the mountain rills,
The beauty of her crowning lights
   Touched all the leaning hills.

Yet strangely while her praises rang,
   Sweet bride of every clime,

Her heart was touched with secret pang—
   The pain of parting time.

So on the sunward slopes awhile
   She paused and waved her hand,
And going, left her parting smile
   Upon the autumn land.

AN OLD STORY RETOLD.

Well sang the bard in verse sublimely true
That "distance lends enchantment to the view;"
He might have added in the self-same tone
That she had never yet returned the loan!
So by this spell through hazy years remote
She hides the glories of a ragged coat,
And shows to us through leagues of crystal air,
Some howling waste, as Eden, sweet and fair!

But when she takes some bit of common clay
With spirit rife and full of passion's play,
And bids us look through purple reaches dim
To see the glories conjured by her whim
About this mortal so exalted grown,
Whose stature now so far exceeds our own,—
Just wipe your glasses—shade your dazzled eyes—
The second look may check your first surprise!

Reflect a moment: through the endless range
Of years and ages, most things seem to change:
While star and sphere are through the spaces whirled,
And throb of earthquake trembles round the world,—
Tides, seasons, mountains, and the sea that binds

AN OLD STORY RETOLD.

Are shifting always as the changeful winds,
One thing is changeless—on this rolling ball
Old human nature holds its own through all!

This fact assured, then keep within your ken
That boys are only little less than men;
That past or present, whether bond or free
A boy's a boy—at least he's apt to be.
This statement true becomes the key of gold
To this old story which is here retold.

Great was the man who seemed so wisely sent
To lead our armies—be our president!
Not simply great in manhood he appears,
But great in boyhood's young and guileless years
He owned a hatchet, so the story goes—
You know the legend everybody knows,—
And how his father had a cherry tree,
Graceful and tall and beautiful to see.
One day our youth while busy hacking round
Fell on this tree, and cut it to the ground!
Now when he saw his father coming out
He hid his hatchet 'neath his roundabout,
And when 'twas asked, who made the tree to fall?
He didn't know, nor could he guess at all,
But he surmised some colored youth somewhere
Had cut it down to get the cherries there!
This boy was trying now, as well he might,
To keep the hatchet from his father's sight;
But while he circled cautiously around
At last he dropped the weapon on the ground!
Ah! sad indeed! His was a piteous plight,
With all his chances higher than a kite!
Here might we pause, for doubtless on his part

His father spoke the fullness of his heart;
Then reaching down he plucked a lithe, long shoot,
That grew in beauty from a hickory root,
And touched the youth in such a magic way
It turned his dark forgetfulness to day!
And knowing now who made the tree to fall,
He spoke the truth and told his father all!—
Kind friends take warning—do not reason why,
But like our hero, never tell a lie!

OLD AND NEW.

While Midnight, with ensandaled feet
Walked the star-paved upper street,
Clad in her jewels rich and rare,
With dust of diamonds in her hair,
A bent and weary pilgrim old
Went shivering through the dreary cold,
With haggard face of pain upturned,
That through the darkness looked and yearned
For his lost youth : but when the clang
Of joy-bells through the arches rang,
He passed from sight. With radiant frame
An angel form of beauty came
And took his place. His eyes were wet
With tender tears of sweet regret;
But, kissed by Midnight's calm content,
Adown the starry arch he went;
And Morn swung wide her gates and smiled
Upon the New Year undefiled.

IN SPRINGTIME.

Spring comes above the barren world
    By winter ruled so long,
And where his snows were lately hurled
    Sits April's life and song.

Through all the forest branches wide
    She wakes the vital flood—
The burly chestnut's rugged tide,
    The maple's amber blood.

She gives her blessing to the buds
    Down all the sylvan ways;
And bursting into green, the woods
    Fling out their airy sprays.

From greening tints on all things laid
    In wayward curve and line,
The swarthy hemlock takes a shade,
    The needles of the pine.

The alders drop their golden dust,
    The willows wave and gleam,
The lichens blotch the rocks with rust,
    The snow-drops bloom and dream.

Sweet forms of beauty manifold
    Are brought on April's wing:—
The spice-bush's threaded beads of gold
    On budded branches cling.

Above the gray rock's hem of moss
    The wind-flower nods and turns;

The vines of goldthread run across,
    The flaming pinxter burns.

By quiet pool and foaming run
    The silken ferns unfurl,
And shining laurel drinks the sun
    From tinted cups of pearl.

Where summer's faded leaves are laid
    To rest in quiet dells,
The trailing mayflower twines her braid
    And hangs her sweetest bells.

On sunward slopes that downward reach
    To meadow-lands below,
The clouds of apple-bloom and peach
    Are drifting like the snow.

Warm sunshine wooes the springing grain
    To crown the waiting farms,
And God gives by His sun and rain
    The sheaves for Autumn's arms.

So Spring-time keeps her league with earth,
    And sweet flowers bloom and nod,—
From death springs life to fairest birth,
    To keep our faith in God.

PETER COOPER.

God's gracious hand in silent tenderness
    But touched the brow that age had wrinkled
        deep,
    And weary care made way for blessed sleep,

And peace immortal crowned his faithfulness!
No more the years his silvered hair will press:
   His work, well wrought, shall unborn thousands
      cheer,
Who, weary toiling in the twilight here,
Shall teach their lips his honored name to bless.
So shall he live, loved by his fellow-man,—
   In true affection held forever young:
No shaft is needed for a name so pure.
   His deed and thought were part of God's own
      plan:
Though brazen fame may give his name no tongue,
   His work shall live, approved, accepted, sure!

THE CHILDREN'S DAY.

To-day within these leafy shades
   'Mid graceful columns springing,
What happy voices stir the glades
   And blend with nature's singing:—
The glad leaves murmur mellow trills,
   The birds their notes are trying,
And echoes from the breezy hills
   Are glad in their replying.

'Tis well to leave the dusty street,
   Its busy cares foregoing,—
To hear the pulse of nature beat
   And feel her breezes blowing:—
For always she has songs to cheer,
   The lowliest heart upraising,
If we but lend to her an ear,
   To hear her reverent praising.

God's voice is in the grove we tread,
    We hear its whispered sweetness,—
His presence as the leaves o'erhead
    Bends o'er our incompleteness:
And rosy childhood wears once more
    The touch of His caressing,
As on Judea's hills of yore
    He crowned it with His blessing.

Since this is childhood's holiday,
    Let every lip be smiling,
And care and sorrow flee away
    From every heart's beguiling:—
For ere they reach the wished-for years
    Where lie the golden meadows,
Perchance will spring the fount of tears
    And fall the woven shadows!

We cannot bid the years remain,
    Or stay in all their going,—
Too brief indeed is childhood's reign,
    Too swift the time is flowing;
But we may lend a kindly hand,
    Or lift a gentle warning,
To make the paths of wonderland
    All glorious as the morning!

We all are pilgrims old or young,
    Forever onward faring;—
Some cheer the way with songful tongue
    And some go on uncaring;—
Some far ahead see lights of home,
    Some stray in tangled wildwood,
While far below the children roam
    The sunny vale of childhood!

A wondrous valley neath the skies !—
    We all have known its winding :—
How nearer fairy-land it lies
    Than any after finding !
A storied realm, where false and fair
    Claim equal faith out-reaching,
Where wierdest forms that dreams may wear
    Are true as any preaching !

Alas ! when once we pass the vale
    There is no backward turning,
Howe'er the dreams of life may fail,
    Howe'er the heart be yearning :
But still its garnered wealth we hold
    Though far beyond the portal,
And more than royal stores of gold,
    Its memories immortal !

O pictures ! hanging evermore
    Upon the walls unfading,
How time re-touches o'er and o'er
    Each tender tint and shading !
Fair treasures held in endless tryst !—
    Alas ! in Eden's wildwood,
What glory Eve and Adam missed
    Without a gleam of childhood !

Of mother's power to soothe and bless,
    Her smile above them leaning,
Of cradle song and sweet caress
    They never knew the meaning !
How much was lost from living then
    With childhood yet unrisen ;—
No Daniel in the lion's den,
    Nor Joseph in the prison !

Alas! they knew no Jacob's dream,
   Low on a stone reclining,
With golden ladder's lifted gleam
   And angels white and shining!
How David slew the giant strong,
   The hosts of God defying,
Or how he soothed with harp and song
   Saul's demon yet undying!

And yet with childhood's tales untold,
   No sunny gleams returning,
They lived and loved, grew gray and old,
   And never knew its yearning.
But fondly yet our memory clings
   To tides still backward flowing,
While light as from an angel's wing
   Is waved above their going.

Fair childhood wears a diadem
   Unknown in song or story
Since One was born at Bethlehem
   Who crowned it with His glory:
And when He came the angels told
   In song the wondrous stranger,
And wise men came with gifts of gold
   To worship at a manger!

Since in that far Judean land
   He gave His tenderest blessing
To childhood 'neath his loving hand,
   In warm and sweet caressing;
Since by the open gates of Nain
   He changed to joy the weeping,—
Or woke a tender maid again
   From death's still dreamless sleeping;—

Since Galilean mothers brought
    To him their babes, revealing
The depths of mother love, and sought
    For them his touch of healing,—
How fairer far the world has grown
    Through grace of His adorning,
How far good-will to man has flown
    Since that first Christmas morning!

So childhood wears a fadeless crown,
    And cloudless o'er it glowing
The skies of morn are bending down,
    And breath of bloom is blowing;
And when our years of wandering flee—
    We gain the golden portal—
Perchance one joy of Heaven will be
    That childhood is immortal!

ON READING AN OLD POET.

A NIGHT of storm! The blinding flakes are blown
    By frost-stung winds that smite the trees and moan.
The leafless branches creak amid the cold,
    While winter's storm-march sweeps the drifted wold.
The casement rattles—on the window pane
    A fairy artist builds Aladdin's fane—
A wondrous palace crowned with gleaming spires,
    Whose opal windows blaze with diamond fires!

Without, the storm's wild tumult and its din,—
    Thy gladsome song makes melody within,

While on the hearth the wood-fire's blaze and glow
  Defies the gale and laughs at drifting snow!

We own thy charm, and lo! the cagēd birds
  Are hushed to hear the music of thy words;
And more and more thy woven spell holds sway
  And haunts the night with visions of the day,
By mellow songs with matchless grace replete
    And love's own rapture throbbing warm and sweet,
To whose rare music swelling full and clear
  The storm drifts by, and lo! the stars appear!

TO E. A. B.

O FRIEND immortal in the summer land!
  I fain would greet thee as in days of old,
  Whose thronging memories me to-night enfold,
And know again thy friendly grasp of hand.
The tidal years touch not thy golden strand,
  Nor steal the strength of manhood's early prime;
  The shore unshadowed knows no passing time,
For life immortal hath no shifting sand.
O, loyal heart, what greetings manifold
  Beyond the borders shall our spirits share?
  When sundering years have parted for awhile!
Thy shadow dim within my hand I hold;
  Nor can I doubt that in the morning air
  Our clasping hands will wake the olden smile.

OCTOBER.

  At morn the white mist fills
  The valleys rimmed with hills.
  Above the meadows shorn,

And ripened shocks of corn,—
Above the quiet streams,
Scarce wakened from the dreams
Of stars they saw in sleep,
The snowy garments sweep,
Till sunbeams, fold on fold,
Roll back the mist in gold,
To show how glad earth lies
Beneath October's skies.

A dreamy golden haze
Fills up the autumn days.
Wild asters linger yet
With ragged briars thick set,
And o'er the land far blown
The thistle-down is sown.
Round old trees moss-enshrined,
Where bitter-sweet is twined,
Its coral berries press
Against the sun-bright dress,
Like rustic beads and charms
On beauty's neck and arms.

The frost-grape's clusters shine
Along the rambling vine
Half hid by russet sprays
Tangled in lawless ways
With branches wooed and won
To lift them to the sun.

Rare sunsets burning low
Transfigure in their glow
To garbs divinely fair,
The robes the woodlands wear.

The chestnut's changing crown
Is dropping bright leaves down,
And frosted burs spread wide
Their bearded globes of pride,
And let the brown nuts blow
To waiting hands below.

The hazels close beside
Are jeweled like a bride,
And stand aglow with bliss
Beneath October's kiss.
The maples change their dress
Of summer loveliness
For hues that quickly fade
Into a richer shade,
Till satisfied they blaze
In saintly robes of praise.

When autumn gales appear,
Singing the waning year,
Then all the woodland grieves
At loss of summer leaves,
Wind-swept in drifting herds,
Like flocks of golden birds,
While shadows thinner grow
On russet slopes below.

At last her work is done,
October's race is run.
The early promise sent
Has reached accomplishment:
Her ripened harvests told
Amid her brown and gold,
She takes her rest awhile
Wearing her patient smile,

While stubble fields lie bare
In hazy autumn air.

Mr. McGREGOR.

(July 23, 1885.)

It was morning on the mountains,
  And the faintest flush of day
Stole in across the tree-tops,
  And kindled far away:
Then the weary eyes grew brighter
  As the curtains were withdrawn,
And afar they looked and waited
  For the glory of the dawn.

But coming in its beauty,
  With crimson and with gold,
The eyes were all too weary
  Its brightness to behold:
And when the growing splendor
  Poured its glory over all,
It was morning on the mountains
  Where the shadows never fall!

A SONG IN THE NIGHT.

At midnight wakened from unquiet sleep
  By troubled dreams and pain,
I heard through darkness measureless and deep,
  The music of the rain.

Day after day the earth had waited long
  In speechless stress of prayer,

And ear intent to catch the welcome song
    Now borne upon the air.

No dew had cooled the tender grass at morn
    The web the spider spun,
Of all its wealth of beaded beauty shorn,
    Long rusted in the sun.

The clouds of promise only brought despair:
    The corn leaves crisply rolled,
Long since had drained the dew's sweet jewels rare,
    Like pleasure's queen of old.

My troubled heart was full of doubt and fear
    And trust did almost die:
Did God regard, and would he ever here
    Again our feeble cry?

But while I slept there came the blessed rain—
    The boon withheld so long—
In crystal murmurs over hill and plain,
    And filled the air with song!

And while the music stirred the forest leaves
    And through the darkness swept,
The nested birds beneath my dripping eaves
    Chirped out their praise and slept.

Their notes recalled the old words sweet and true—
    The words the Master said—
He feedeth them: and trust sprang up anew,
    And doubt forever fled.

SUGAR-TIME.

Old winter wheels his sullen flight
   Above the brown, uncovered hills,
While budding alders feel the pulse
   And hear the songs of hidden rills.

Still earth, the sleeping beauty, lies
   Half conscious, dreaming, while she turns,
And waits the sunshine's princely kiss,
   For which her drowsy being yearns.

The brown eaves drop their crystal rain
   In songful murmurs till the night
Hangs low a fringe of icy spears
   Inlaid with stars and barbed with light.

Now all the woodlands feel the spell
   Of waning dark and climbing sun,
And fragrant birch and whispering pine
   Are thrilled with quickened pulses won.

The maples dream of autumn's gold
   Transmuted under winter snows,
Till all their wealth of amber blood
   In honeyed sweetness overflows.

AT LAST.

As drifting shadows leave no sign
   Each rounded year,
How many pass the border line,
   And disappear!

For each is set a certain bound—
  A course to run;
And when the utmost goal is found,
  All work is done.

Somewhere the shadow cuts the light
  Across each way,
And there the starry, solemn night
  Will close the day.

How far away the hilltops rise
  Where *finis* stands,
Where dreamless sleep will close our eyes,
  And fold our hands,

It matters not;—or near, or far,
  Alike are they:
The hand that guides the sweeping star
  Will lead the way.

What though we glimpse through misty air
  Some empty nest,—
No atom drifts beyond His care,—
  His time is best.

As shadows sweep the summer hills
  And vanish then,
Each life some rounded purpose fills,—
  Threescore, or ten.

And when our work has grown complete,
  Our triumph won,
We shall abide where rest is sweet,
  When work is done.

CHIPPEWANOXETTO.

A SCANTY pasture slope of brown
   Where stunted bushes grow,
A ragged coast-line beaten down
   By storm and tidal flow;

A fisher's hut, a boat upturned,
   A pile of driftwood near,
And ashen heaps where fires have burned
   To make the noonday cheer;

And southward, stretching like a hand,
   When tides have seaward run,
A slender bar of gray wet sand
   Is bleaching in the sun.

All dreamily they come and go,
   The white sails drifting by—
They fleck the azure sea below
   The broader sweep of sky.

With seaward tides they sail away
   And vanish out of sight,
Beyond the wedge that cleaves the bay,
   And lifts its warning light.

So hangs this picture on my wall,
   A memory of the sea,
While old-time voices seem to call
   The summers back to me.

BIRTHDAY.

A GLOOMY day of winter rain;
   The branches creak, the winds are sad,
The swift drops beat the sodden leaves,

And still the old elm moans and grieves,
But 'tis your birthday once again
   And so my heart is glad.

Dear wife, how brims our cup of joy!
   Your trusting hand in mine I hold:
For while the fleet years spin and run
   Through all the courses of the sun,
To us they bring no base alloy,
   But love's unminted gold!

Far queenlier than a jeweled crown
   Your coronet of silvered hair,
And more and more your love-lit eyes
   Illume for me the darkest skies—
Sweet stars whose clear light beaming down,
   Makes all the waste world fair.

Pass on, O years, with swifter flow!
   We build no more for nesting fears;
But each will find us richer grown
   In all things love has made our own,
And far beyond the after-glow
   Still wait the eternal years!

NATURE'S PLAN.

First the tender leaflet;
   After that appear
The bud and bloom of promise,
   And the ripened ear.

Thus the folded life-germ
   In the acorn found,

Makes the mighty monarch
  Of the forest ground :

And the way-side beauty,
  Growing all the while,
Glads the dusty highway
  With its patient smile.

So the lands are golden
  Neath the sun and rain,
With the yellow billows
  Of the ripened grain.—

What are we the better
  While the seasons flow,
And the years are passing,
  If we do not grow ?—

Grow in all the beauty
  Of the Master's grace
Unto heavenly fruitage
  In our humble place ?

TO HENRY W. LONGFELLOW.

O SONGFUL bard! whose fame the nations hold
Enshrined for aye, thy latest leaves of gold
I turn to-night, and ease an hour of pain
With rarest fancies of the poet's brain.
So passing sweet thy witching spell is wrought
I fain would bless thee for thy pictured thought:
And so I breathe a warm heart's-uttered prayer
For heaven's own blessing on thy snow-white hair,—
That when thy years are rounded full and free

The gates of pearl may inward swing for thee.—
Now could some angel breathe to waiting sense,
The boon I crave hath wrought thee no offence,
What rarer joy would lend its presence sweet
To cheat all pain and make the hour complete.

ON PILGRIMAGE.

The land is fair my footsteps journey through—
A land of promise filled with corn and wine.

Through shaded ways my winding pathway turns
In sweet green pastures by the rills of peace,
Or climbs the slopes where broadening vision sweep
The travelled way to sunrise-smitten hills,
And heights untrod that beckon farther on.

They come and go, the blessed days of peace:
No cloud glooms down but sunshine trembles through
And doubt stays not where patient faith looks up
And takes the good each sweet day holds in store

So on, and on, toward the sunset land
His strong arm leads, and clears the tangled way,
While from His hand unstinted bounty falls,
And undawned splendor brightens far beyond.

AT CEDARCROFT.

With songful heart so still at last
   And brimmed with rest for aye,
He cannot know the shadow cast
   Upon his hills to-day!

So dear, so dear to all the land—
   They loved him young and old,
The generous heart and friendly hand,
   The man of royal mould.

How many homes for him are lone,
   How many eyes are dim,
While winds of winter wail and moan
   A solemn dirge for him.

Sad voices oft his name repeat
   And call for him in vain,
They watch and wait the weary feet
   That never come again.

And one who loves his memory well,
   Looks back through misty tears
Beyond the shadow's woven spell
   Upon the vanished years!

The Kennett hills were robed in green
   And glad with songs of morn,
The valleys wore the meadow's sheen
   And waved with wheat and corn.

The hedgerows made the waysides fair
   Through tangled sun and shade,
Where through the sweet June haunted air
   A dusty pilgrim strayed.

What songs made glad the summer ways
   Of bird and leaf and breeze,
Till Cedarcroft to longing gaze
   Rose 'mid her ancient trees.

The open gate and shadowed way,
    The vine-encumbered wall,
The spacious lawn of bloom and spray,
    With sunset over all!

The kindly words of welcome said,
    The friendly grasp of hand,
They still live on though years have sped
    Since then across the land!

A storm has swept his leafless wood,
    And bowed the monarch forms
Of burly chestnuts which have stood
    A thousand winter storms!

Alas! no more the singing birds!
    The branches wildly toss,
And one he cheered with kindly words
    Is dumb with sense of loss.

TO MY MOTHER ON HER BIRTHDAY.

The brown earth wakens from her dream
    With drowsy pulses low,
While April turns to catch the gleam
    That makes her being glow.

Sunward her quick tides flush and rise
    In raptures warm and sweet,
While mayflowers spring in mute surprise
    Beneath her sandaled feet.

And while she weaves with cunning hand
    The woodland's airy frills,—

A deepening flush across the land,—
　　The green robe of the hills,

Northward she calls her singing throng,
　　Blue bird and thrush and wren,
To greet with glad and mellow song
　　Thy three-score years and ten!

And while she lifts her buds half-blown
　　To deck thy natal day,
All tenderly another stone
　　She sets beside thy way.

On what far slope of tender green
　　The first its shadow cast!
And all thy pathway lies between
　　The earliest and the last!

A changeful way by vale and hill
　　Thy weary feet have run;—
By winding valleys dark and chill,
　　By broad slopes glad with sun!

We need not trace each mile to-day
　　The journey's hopes and fears—
The bloom and blight beside the way,
　　The joys, the smiles, the tears.

Enough that while each glance we steal
　　The shadows flit and fade,
And all the memory lights reveal
　　Far more of light than shade!

To-day, with all the hill-slope fair,
　　Where runs thy pathway down,

We press upon thy silvered hair
   Affection's golden crown.

Be Heaven's broad wealth of blessing thine—
   Fresh manna strew thy way,
For only can some gift divine
   The mother-love repay:

And while the dusky shadows grow
   May sunset still unfold
Across thy way the kindly glow
   From wide-swung gates of gold.

So shall the golden evening-time
   Fairer than morning be,—
Some sweet flush wear of that glad clime
   Where welcome waits for thee.

For while thy natal day we greet,
   What vanished forms appear!—
What long-hushed voices low and sweet
   Fall on thy listening ear!

Perchance where on the hills they stand
   Just veiled from sight away,
Thy birthday on the borderland
   They keep with us to-day!

ONLY FOUR.

O ROSY light of the summer dawn!
   Sweet flush of the kindling skies,
Steal softly over the dewy lawn,
   And touch my darling's eyes.

On the crimson lip and fringèd lid,
  One kiss of thy golden beams
Will open the blue eyes softly hid,
  And call her back from dreams.

And tell her then why the bird-songs sweet
  Ring out so mellow and clear—
Such music as only birds repeat,
  And only birthdays hear.

And how the summers which she has known
  By blossoms of pearl and gold,
Have passed in beauty and quickly flown
  To make her four years old.

Then whisper above my darling's head
  What the tenderest love might say—
What blessings and prayers for her are said
  Who is only four to-day.

For the years to come, O write it down—
  The yearning love and the prayer;
There never can be a richer crown
  For any child to wear.

JUNE.

From tropic lands afar
  She comes with queenly grace,
Serene as any star
  In all the worlds of space;
And in her dreamy eyes
  She bears the blue of summer skies.

Her shining brows are crowned
   With roses sweet and rare,
While half-blown buds are bound
   Amid her waving hair;
And all her beauty's hue
   Is only sunshine staining through.

Her gauzy robes conceal
   In vain her beauty where
Her charms they half reveal;
   Her sun-brown arms are bare,
And in her jewelled hands
   She holds rare gifts for many lands.

Her coming all things know;
   Across the emerald grass
The tiniest flowers that blow
   Look out to see her pass,
While from her sweet face blown
   They catch a glory for their own.

She gives all beauty rare
   Through ages manifold,
Nor ever grows less fair
   Her being's perfect gold;—
All in her matchless truth
   She keeps the peerless grace of youth.

Now fairy-like her tread
   Is on the slopes of green,
Where Summer lifts his head
   Her damasked robes are seen,
And evermore his bride,
   She walks in beauty by his side.

IN WAR TIME.

(1864.)

Bend low through all the Northern land,
   Wild organ forests bend!
Let ocean's voice from strand to strand
   With all your praises blend!

Winds, sweep in might November's skies—
   Her leafless woods and sprays,
Wake all your grandest harmonies,
   And roll them out in praise!

Wild streams and rills and waterfalls!
   Sing while you foam and flow,
Glad praises through your crystal halls
   From lips of pearl and snow!

Leap, praises, on the buglers breath,
   From rifle-pits and caves;
Leap from the cannon's lips of death—
   Ring over nameless graves!

Gleam, sabres, in the growing light—
   Gleam while the trumpet brays,
Wake, drum-beat, through the waning night,
   A nation's song of praise!

Roll out the anthem,—let it swell:
   God reigns!—the wrong shall cease;
Proclaim it, shot, and screaming shell,
   Through broader curves of peace!

All praise to Him!—the ruddy gleams
   Of morning gild the crimson bars

Above our picket's sleepless dreams—
Our country's flag of stars!

TO G. G. B.

To-night, O friend, I greet the stars again,
  Whose kindly light o'er us so long ago,
  Kept patient watch above the hills of snow,
Till flush of morning bade their glory wane!
The self-same stars!—and now my feet would fain
  Reclimb the pass, as on that storm-shut day,
  When night and tempest barred the mountain way—
Save when the cloud-flash lit the spears of rain—
To see once more above the Alpine range
How fair they burned, the storm's wild fury spent,
Flooding the white hills with a beauty strange—
  The ghostly pillars of the firmament!
And with what rapture, their sweet gaze withdrawn,
Mont Blanc's white glory took the kiss of dawn!

LAKE ALBANO.

Fair Alban lake! enzoned with lava gray—
  The red volcano's glowing rim of yore,
  From noon-day rest along thy haunted shore,
We turn to watch thy merry waves at play
Through shade and sunshine of the waning day.
  A winding pathway led our feet to thee
  Along the hillsides, while the distant sea,
Plain, city, mount, and all before us lay.
The palace walls that crowned thy peaceful shore

When Cæsar's city was a thing unborn,
Have crumbled all !—Time leaves a trace no more
Of all the glory of that faded morn !
So fades earth's glory, but the Roman plain,
The sea, the mountains, and thy smile remain !

AN ALPINE LAKE.

From deep unfailing founts that play
   Through sunless rifts below,
Upward the crystal currents stray,—
   The singing waters flow,

Till deep within the blue-walled rim
   Of mountains, azure crowned,
The goblin's granite bowl they brim,
   And here the lake is found.

Alone upon the mountains wild
   It wears its sweetest charms,
And mother Nature owns her child,
   And bears it in her arms !

Fair mirror of the summer heaven
   That bends above its breast,
Or scowling storm of passion driven,
   Across its peace and rest.

The gray old crags with beauty glow
   From its entrancing face,
And distant cones of gleaming snow
   Are grander for its grace.

As fair it smiles as when with blue
   Broad arch above it drawn,

Its virgin freshness woke and knew
  The kisses of the dawn.

No wrinkled trace of age it bears,
  No shadow of decay,
With lilies on its breast it wears
  Its primal youth for aye.

A crystal dream of rest it lies
  By passion's breath unriven,
It holds the brightness of the skies—
  The smile of earth and heaven.

Rare beauty of the lonely wild!
  Who on these heights shall stray,
May leave his care where thou hast smiled,
  And bear thy peace away!

IN THE HAMMOCK.

In the mottled shade of the maple trees,
  Where robin builds and sings,
And the cool leaves shake in the idle breeze
  The children's hammock swings:
Breathe softly, O song of the summer air,
  Bend tenderly down, O sky,
Nor suffer a cloud to darken where
  Three wee, brown maidens lie!

Aloft where the dusk of the twilight dwells,
  The red-breast's hammock swings,
Where the delicate tint of sea-green shells
  Has given place to wings
Come, dreamy and sweet to their noonday rest
  The softest airs that blow,—

To the birds asleep in the robin's nest,
    And brownies asleep below!

ON A FOSSIL SHELL.

Thou ancient mollusk from the oozy deep
    Of vast silurian seas,
I marvel much at thy untroubled sleep
    On such a bed of ease!

What mystic ages have above thee flown!
    Nor is thy slumber past!
Thy plastic couch to bed of sandstone grown
    Still holds thee folded fast!

Since thou so long hast suffered heat and chill,
    The biting frost and rain,
Do not thy stony joints with ague thrill,
    Or sharp rheumatic pain?

What storm and earthquake have about thee
       whirled!—
    How changed the seas their place!—
O sleep no more, but wake and tell the world
    About thy times and race!

Ah! could we know the record of thy reign,
    And all which it befell!
Perchance the heart to-day that beats in pain
    Beat in that age as well!

Thy shell no doubt was rifled ages since
    By some relentless rogue!—
Some kin of ours, perchance a monkey prince
    Were clam-bakes then in vogue?

Or didst thou slake some saurian monsters'
    greed
  In twilights old and gray?—
Thy blameless self some hungry maw to feed,
  Which cast the shell away?

Are not our bivalves still allied to thee
  By long ancestral line?
And haunt they not, as thou, the shallow sea,
  And sip its luscious wine?

Thou speakest not: no answer can we see
  Thy wrinkled visage make,
But still we clasp thy later progeny
  And love them for thy sake!

THE FIRST DECADE.

I.

By the swift years one by one
All the web of life is spun.
Summers come and summers go,
Winters follow with their snow;
Gloom of storm and blue of sky
Mark the seasons passing by;
Song of bird and sunny gleam
Make the long days shorter seem;
Blended sunshine, sport and play,
Chase the winged hours away,
Till thy rounded years have made
Life's eventful first decade!

II.

So the summers passing fair
Over childhood free from care,
Leading vales of dreamland through—
Fairy valleys wet with dew,
Full of sweet enchantment grand,
Making life a wonderland,—
These have vanished while thy feet
Treading roses, rare and sweet,
All unconsciously have run
Through the shadow and the sun,
Till the changing seasons say
Thou art ten years old to-day!

III.

Here upon the border line
What a legacy is thine!
Better far than treasured wealth
Dew of youth and rosy health:
Eyes to see the beauty spread
All around and overhead,
Ears to hear the music sung
Not alone by lip and tongue,
Heart to feel and mind to know
How His bounties overflow,
Richer far than fable old,
Better than the touch of gold!

IV.

Therefore let the golden days
Touch thy lips with grateful praise,
Wreath thy brow with patient smile,

Keep thy tender heart from guile:
So may all the graces shine
In those dreamful eyes of thine;
Faith look up with vision clear
Far beyond the utmost sphere;
Hope with soaring pinion strong
Lift thee on the wings of song,
While the swift years drift away
Under Love's benignant sway.

v.

All the years, which lie before
Wait to bless thee with their store:
Wealth of treasure, riches rare,
These may be thy portion fair.
Gladly face each rising sun
With the peace of duty done:
Let each sunset's fading glow
Note how love's sweet roses grow,
With divinest fragrance rife,
Sweetening all the toils of life:
So at last shall rest be sweet
When the last decade's complete!

IN THE SOUDAN.

GORDON! a name to thrill
The heart of the valiant still.
Noble and true and tender,
In the dust of Egypt's splendor,
Marred by hostile spears,
Mourned by a nation's tears,
The great commander lies
Under the desert skies.

A soldier whose fame has flown
Where'er the winds have blown.
How shall we tell the story
Rehearsing his deeds of glory?
How fair white honor crowned him,
And all the graces found him?

Though dead by the slumberous stream,
That winds through Egypt's dream,
Where the tropic palms will wave
Forever above his grave,
The winds of the desert moan
For the valiant spirit flown,
And never his fame can be hid
In the land of the pyramid.

What deeds of valor done
'Neath the tropic's burning sun!
The march of weary feet
Through the desert's blinding heat,
The siege at last and the doom
By the walls of far Khartoum—
The pride of the stream which flows
From Kenia's lifted snows,
Watched ever by palm and star
From the crags of Ankobar.

O city he held so long
With a few brave hearts and strong,
Where he swept with gracious sway
Oppression and wrong away,
Betrayed by the foe and lost
At such a perilous cost!

So perished three hundred men
Of old in a mountain glen!
All marred by hostile spears
And mourned by a nation's tears,
The dead commander lies
Under Egypt's haunted skies!

ORION.

My room is darkened: through the window bars
   Orion's light in unspent beauty burns,
  As mailed in might he toils above nor turns
To note the calm procession of the stars:
With lofty purpose crowned and grim with scars,
   The war club in his brawny hand he bears,
   The slaughtered lion's shaggy skin he wears—
Type of the passion which the white soul mars.
And still he smites in his heroic wrath
   The tossing horns that hedge his upward way,
Till every form of evil in his path
   Bows low, at last, to his unchallenged sway.
And from the stars a clear voice rings, "Be strong!
Thou too shalt conquer in the strife with wrong!"

PONTE ST. ANGELO.

Beneath the stars that watch the Tiber's flow,
   Slow winding through the glory of a dream—
   The hush of midnight on the haunted stream—
I pace the ancient bridge, St. Angelo!
The years in sooth have stained its marble snow
   And dimmed the beauty of its early prime,
   Yet still it hears the passing centuries chimes,

Its strength unmarred as in the mornings glow !—
O Roman splendor throned upon the hills!
    O dream of empire over every clime!
How burns the heart thy classic story thrills,
    How pale thy glories in the lapse of time !
Thy kings are dust ; thy royal pageants flee ;
St. Angelo remains and Tiber seeks the sea !

ROUND LAKE.

Long ages since when earth was new,
    One glad and golden morn,
Beneath the bending arch of blue
    The forest lake was born.

Earth cradled it among her hills,
    The clouds gave blessing sweet,
And green slopes sent the laughing rills
    To bathe its crystal feet.

What beauty bent above its dreams
    While ages rolled away !
By night the stars with tender gleams
    The golden sun by day.

The rosy flush of kindling dawn,
    The brighter glow of even,
The clouds across the azure drawn
    The sunset fires of heaven.

Alone amid the wilderness
    Its perfect grace it wore,
And kept its beauty none the less
    Of pictured sky and shore.

Unseen, until the savage strayed
   Unhindered through the wild,
Round Lake, enzoned with forest shade,
   Looked up to heaven and smiled.

Here paused the Indian by its side
   When shades of evening fell,
And hither came his dusky bride
   To braid her tresses well.

And here she found what nature gave
   For her adornment fair—
The water-lilies from the wave
   To dress her raven hair.

The red man here in speechless mood,
   Adored with bended form,
The spirit of the pathless wood,
   Of sunshines and of storm.—

Swift years of changing beauty throng,
   And fairest years unclose
The wilderness alive with song,
   And blossomed as the rose.

For Art has laid her soft caress
   On Nature's wayward child,
And won by force of tenderness
   The rude and rugged wild.

Beside the lake's unruffled peace
   Green walled with hills around,
Are groves whose shadows bring release
   From Care's enchanted ground.

The broad encampment's winding streets
   Mid haunt of breeze and bird,
Cool shaded parks and dusk retreats
   With songs of fountains heard.

The gleam of white tents in the shade,
   By sunshine mottled fair,
And under dark green branches swayed
   The cottage homes of prayer.

Where erst the Indian's stealthy feet
   Roamed through the forest ways,
God's greenwood temple stands complete,
   And sounding with his praise,

Through all its airy arches hung
   Leaf-fretted 'neath the blue,
What melodies of heaven are rung,
   What music trembles through!

The songs of pilgrim worshippers
   In blended triumph rolled,
The forest's-anthem as it stirs
   Its branches mossed with gold.

The voice of prayer and praises given,
   The Master's echoed words,
Down ringing from the rest of heaven,
   And gladdest songs of birds.

Since first he built the spacious arch
   Of blue above the land,
And stars and suns began their march
   To music sweet and grand,

No marble fane of praise and prayer,
  In vast cathedral dim
With vaulted aisles has seemed more fair
  Than forest grove to Him.

As in the olden years again
  In shadowy glade and glen,
He whom the heavens cannot contain
  Vouchsafes to dwell with men.

And though unseen, above we know
  The ladder's starry rounds,
On which His angels come and go
  Above the tented grounds.

And this is Bethel whose green walls
  Ascending praises fill,
Where healing flows and manna falls
  And God abideth still.

THANKSGIVING.

(1866)

Put off, O earth, thy faded dress,
  Put on thy garb of beauty,
And in thy robes of righteousness
  Stand forth arrayed for duty.

Hush every note of hate and wrong—
  Each bitter wail of sadness;
Let all thy voices swell one song
  Of love and praise and gladness.

Wild winter storms that sift your snows
  Above the withered daisies,

Wake all your strength from its repose
   And storm the heavens with praises.

O Land, bow lowly in the dust
   The while ye lift your voices,—
God has but smitten where he must,
   And Liberty rejoices.

Each peaceful grave where valor sleeps
   In loyal rest unbroken,
Shall be to every eye that weeps
   Our sins' perpetual token.

Praise Him ye vales of fair renown
   Whose wrath your slopes has rifted,
Praise Him ye hills above whose crown
   The battle smoke has drifted.

Praise Him ye men of loyal might—
   Your gleaming eyes grow brighter,
Through God your arm has kept the right;—
   The world is growing lighter!

Praise Him, O man, that in thy soul
   Lacked faith for right endeavor—
God reigneth while the seasons roll,
   And He shall reign forever!

KEATS' GRAVE.

Thy leaf is withered but thy sweetness stays
   Dear Pansy, grown where frown the ancient walls
Above his grave, and gloom of cypress falls

Across the sunshine of the Roman days:
Plucked long ago, I hold thee still in praise
   Of him whose song full soon to silence grew—
   Whose glorious morning faded with the dew
Yet lives immortal in his mellow lays!
Not writ in water, nay, the swift years bring
   But added lustre to his shining name :—
Forever young, untouched by passing wing,
   His broken threads of song are dear to fame!
Green is his grave from tears of love untold,
While English daisies star the grass with gold!

TO OLIVER WENDELL HOLMES.

A Christmas greeting tangled in a rhyme
   I give for sunshine on the clouded years—
   For wholesome laughter brewing tender tears,
For words of cheer that gladden manhood's prime!
O world-wide Singer! deem it not a crime,
   Since thy sweet songs have made so many glad,
   If one should sing not in the song-robes clad,
And utter praise ill put and out of time.—
Sweet peace be thine upon this Christmas-day
   To lengthen out for thee life's lessening span,
   To quicken good and laugh the bad away,
With merry heart that doeth good to man!
   God bless thee now, and if I do thee wrong
   Yet love I none the less the Singer and his song.

RAVENSWOOD.

O classic shades of Ravenswood,
   Thy memory holds them fast;—

Enfold them now, one brotherhood,
    The children of the past!

To-day the years anew will blow—
    The coast of life will loom,
And olden times stand all aglow
    In memory's light and bloom.

Wave all thy shadows cool and sweet
    To lure the feet that roam,
While words of kindly welcome greet
    The wanderer's coming home.

O tender smile of June bend low
    From cloudless deeps of air—
Breathe softly summer winds, and blow
    Thy welcome everywhere.

They come from far—they hear the call
    Borne out upon the breeze—
From far and near they gather all
    Round Alma Mater's knees.

Not now as in the days of old,
    When with their bashful tread,
They came at first through heat and cold
    Where homesick tears were shed,

But gladly now do they appear—
    The old-time girls and boys;
They come and bring their children here,—
    The precious household joys!

Ah! how the busy years have run
    Their swift and silent way,—

'Tis noon and past, by many a sun,
  For some are turning gray!

God bless you friends and comrades true!
  His bounty on you fall,
While faded dreams of life anew
  Come sweet and fresh to all.

And well may those whom fate denies
  To join the welcome band,
Look forth to-day from misty eyes,
  And clasp each friendly hand!

Ah yes, for where the coast is fair
  And fresh with foam and spray,
And white sails gleam in summer air
  Upon the broad blue bay,

Two loyal hearts who treasure well
  Life's visions as they should,
Greet olden friends to-day and dwell
  On scenes of Ravenswood!

They muse on all the vanished years,
  Rich memories held in store,
And while the shifting past appears
  They count the pictures o'er.

Ah, how in memory's light they blend
  Each faded tint and line,
With smile of each remembered friend
  Inwrought in the design.

Again they send you words of cheer
  From far New England's strand :—

To all in memory held so dear
   They reach the clasping hand.

And well they know how on the green
   Where many fondly stray,
A presence felt, but all unseen,
   Walks in your midst to-day!

The suns of many years have set—
   We've journeyed many a mile,
And still we hold, nor can forget
   Her old remembered smile!

And others swell unseen the throng,
   Or linger fondly near—
To old familiar words of song
   They lend a willing ear.

We may not clasp the viewless hand,
   Nor bid them speak, or stay,
But still unbroken is the band,
   Nor they are near to-day!

They linger still,—they are not dead;
   And when the years are passed,
In grand reunion just ahead,
   We all shall meet at last!

MY INHERITANCE.

ALL meanly as one lowly born,
   Though noble blood was mine,
I took the ways of doubt and scorn
   Heir of a royal line!

And forth in far unfriendly lands
    My wayward feet did roam,
Through desert wastes and burning sands
    Afar from peace and home.

Above me spread no palm-wide wings
    Across the blinding way;—
No shade of rocks, no cooling springs
    To cheer my lonely way.

My garb was utter wretchedness
    That wrapped me round and round,
And only want and weariness
    In all the land was found.

If seeming rest remote and far
    Did lure as something fair,
At last it fled, a mocking star,
    Through hot, illusive air.

And hope each passing year grew less,
    The desert seemed more wide,
And all its joys were emptiness—
    Its dreans unsatisfied.

So broadly stretched the weary waste
    Unfanned by angel wing,
Till one day came to me in haste
    A message from the king!

What gladsome news to one so vile!
    How fled my doubt and care!
The king had loved me all the while
    And made me now his heir!

The title-deed to wealth untold,
    With royal seal and sign,
My eager hands now grasp and hold—
    Its treasures all are mine!

I pause not here to count them o'er,
    My wealth transcends all thought,
Though grasping ever more and more,
    The wealth that Love hath wrought!

No more I tread the desert sand
    Nor look through blinding tears,—
Co-heir of heaven and earth I stand,
    And the eternal years!

CHRISTMAS.

FAR from Eastern lands and climes,
First to hear the angel chimes
From the walls of sapphire flung,
From the towers of jasper rung,—
From the hills where listening long
Shepherds caught the wondrous song
"Peace on earth,"—the Christ is born,—
"Good will to men:"—from thence the morn
That smote the dusky slopes with praise,
Dawns now as in the olden days.

O welcome day, O welcome morn—
Good will to men, for Christ is born!
From the steeples high in air
Ring, O bells, ring everywhere,
Till the music throbs and thrills
Through the valleys, o'er the hills;—

On the woodlands bare and brown,
The crowded mart, the busy town,
Ring the joyous welcome down!

Come thou morn of song and mirth,
Make glad the white-robed, waiting earth.
Spread all thy treasures far and near,
Make all hearts warm, dry every tear.
Bring thou afresh to every thought
The living words divinely taught,
The deeds of love the Master wrought.
Let that glad song the angels sung
With trembling harp and glowing tongue,
Find answer in the self-same words,
That woke of old the golden chords,
And sweetly from the shining wall
Came down to earth—"Good will to all."

We hail thy dawn!—bring cheer to men
And warm the old year's heart again.
With snowy locks December stands
Mid sleet and storm;—his wasted hands
A frosty scepter grasp and hold,—
His frame is bent, his limbs are old,—
His bearded lips are iced and pale,
He shivers in the winter gale.
Come then, O day of warm heart-cheer,
Make glad the waste and waning year,
While old December shivering goes
To rest beneath the drifted snows!

IN PEACE.

Across the dewy hills of dawn
    The bugle call is blown;
Why leap the echoes through the morn
    When clouds of war have flown?

A sweeter strain than rang of old
    'Mid war's discordant bray,
It calls from mellow throat of gold
    In camps of peace to-day;

Broad fields where rest in wave-like flow,
    O'er-run by summer's sheen,
With foamy spray of bud and blow,
    The silent tents of green.

Through crowded ranks along the sward,
    By unfrequented ways,
We pass unchallenged by the guard,
    With flowers of love and praise.

From fields that drank the warm red rain
    Their valor won release,—
No bugle call can break again
    Their golden dream of peace.

AT DAWN.

All tired of life and full of weariness,
  How oft we come to blessed night's repose
  And 'neath the veil that sleep about us throws,
Lose all our cares in sweet forgetfulness.
So far removed from busy jar and stress

While sleep rebuilds the wasted tower of strength,
  We scarce believe when morning dawns at length,
The stars have trod their round of watchfulness!
  So when we waken full of rest at last
    In matchless glory of the cloudless dawn—
This earthly span of being over-past,
    Its luring phantoms evermore withdrawn,—
  Refreshed by airs of that diviner sphere,
How like a vanished dream will all the past appear!

APRIL DAYS.

April morning rich and rare,
Sunrise glory in the air,
Birds of song are on the wing,
Ah, the melodies they bring.
Through the quiet morning hush
Note of sparrow, song of thrush,
When the robin's strain of praise
And the blue-bird's liquid lays;
Sweet the peewee's song and then
The nervous twitter of the wren.

All the woodlands feel again
The touch of April sun and rain.
On the forest slopes are seen
Nature's softest tints of green;
Bursting buds are here and there
Waving in the golden air,
Tufted plumes and fairy frills
Seen against the leaning hills.
Buds that hid in many a fold
Petals of the rarest gold,
Tints of azure or of flame,

Foam or flush of maiden shame
Now reveal their wealth between
    Bursting bodices of green.

    Where the runnel's winding ways
Gurgle under budding sprays,
And its limpid crystal drips
O'er the ledge's mossy lips,
Gladdening all the quiet glooms
There the alder hangs its plumes,
And the drooping willow grows
Greener where its laughter flows.

In the dells are lifted up
Many a sweet and tender cup,
Where the timid wild-flowers grow
By the lingering drifts of snow;
'Neath the dead leaves hidden, twines
The modest mayflower's rustic vine,
While its blooms in glad surprise,
Look up to the April skies,—
Sweetest wild-flowers wooed and won
By the fickle April sun.
All the hosts of growing things
Feel a stirring as of wings,
And are wakened from their dreams
By the warm and sunny gleams
Of April sunshine in the air,—
Springtime's splendor everywhere.

SOME AFTER-SUPPER LINES.

I MET a man the other day
    Whose face with rapture beamed,

I wish that all were half as glad
   As that dear fellow seemed;—
He took me kindly by the hand,
   His smile was gay and light,
And whispered, "Would I come and see
   The Philos feast to-night?"

I shook my head—I couldn't tell—
   And then he opened wide
His bearded lips and said, "Of course
   You'll feast yourself beside!"—
That settled it:—I'd truly come!—
   Perhaps you may have heard
Some one regret the famine here
   Because I kept my word!

But back of this I queried well
   What fare might here be had;
In sooth to say, I learned too much,
   It only made me sad.
Who could but grieve at such a time,—
   His eyes with sorrow fill,
That prosy speech must end the day,
   That toast was on the bill?

"Of course," he said, "You'll make a speech,
   And write it out with care,
Impromptu things will never do
   For this high-toned affair!"
And furthermore he grieved to say,
   Then closed his eyes and sighed,
"The Philos think a joke is green
   Unless it's cut and dried!"

Since then I've racked my weary brain,
    While fancy wandered far,
In search of some propitious trail
    Beneath some kindly star.
But thought won't always come at will
    No more than cream will rise
On milk already skimmed to death
    And blue as April skies!

You'll find it thus,—the sprites that keep
    Thought's spindles whirling round,
Will sometimes take a holiday,
    Not one can then be found!
Then though it be a song, or joke,
    Or speech, or what you will,
No grist can then be ground because
    No sprite will turn the mill!

Who has not mourned when all too late
    His faulty prose or rhyme,
The brilliant things he might have said
    If he had thought in time?
So when this feast is fully past
    And all the mischief done,
The merry sprites will homeward flock,
    And turn the mill for fun!

Most surface things are flat and stale,—
    This doubtless you may know,—
But still we have to take the foam
    To get the undertow.
The rarest thought comes always late,
    I had no time to borrow,—

Please try this banquet o'er again,
And call on me to-morrow!

AT THE GATE.

Down through the skies, from Heaven's portal straying,
  In beauteous guise she came,
Nor long enough her term of earthly staying
  To take a shade of blame.

The summer voices caught a note of sweetness
  From her first spoken words,—
Far richer, sweeter, in their full completeness,
  Our darlings than the birds.

Where morning dwells is always golden brightness—
  She was our household dawn;
Fairer she grew than lily in its whiteness,
  Till from our sight withdrawn.

Astray from Heaven, the angel love supernal
  Through her brief absence yearned,
Till calling her they crowned with life eternal
  Her brow when she returned.

And now she lives the blessed life immortal,—
  Though tears will fall above her—
Forever safe within the golden portal,
  Where still the angels love her.

Somewhere our way shall brighten like the dawning

When dusky night has flown,
And we shall greet the ever-cloudless morning
And clasp again our own!

Meanwhile the years grow weary with delaying,
The years that we must wait,
Till far beyond the shadows, Heavenward straying.
We meet her at the gate.

TO JOHN G. WHITTIER.

O MINSTREL crowned with snow-white years,
And praised by many a tongue;
How many eyes forget their tears
For words which thou hast sung.

How ring for right and truth thy lays
Along the toilful past,
What sunshine upon shadowed ways
Thy mellow songs have cast.

For briars of doubt and thorns of care
That weave a tangled maze,
Thy calm sweet faith and hopeful prayer
Have given flowers of praise.

For me, O poet, song arrayed,
The charm thy words impart,
Like singing birds of June have made
Glad summer in my heart.

And still I hold, though years will pass
Thy smile and cheer that day,
'Mid waving shadows on the grass,
And breath of new-mown hay.

O restful hour!—how swift it sped:
  But when I left thy door,
My doubtful starlight overhead
  Had turned to dawn once more!

So while the waning years depart
  Across the winter snow,
Thy words of welcome in my heart
  Make cheerful afterglow.

  breathe thy words:—His ear will heed
    The prayer by love upborne,—
That Heaven will down the slope still lead
  As up the hills of morn."

Yea, more for thee my heart would claim,
  But lip and tongue forbear,
My fairest speech would fail to frame
  The still unuttered prayer.

One boon I crave:—forgive to-night
  What best had been untold;—
The head may err,—the heart is right,
  And love is sometimes bold.

OUR REFUGE.

Though guiding suns and systems in their flight
  Through realms sublimely fair,
No earth-born atom drifts beyond the sight
  Of His most tender care.

No trill grows silent in the sparrow's song,
  Nor timid eye grows dim,

No lily pales amid the meadow throng
  But it is known of Him.

He is our refuge;—safe on either hand,
  By noonday, or by night,
No pestilence can smite us where we stand,
  Nor poisoned arrow's flight.

His presence wraps us like a garment round;
  Together day by day
We journey on, while sweeter streams abound
  And fairer grows the way.

ENFRANCHISED.

It comes at last, so long delayed,
  By red ways battle-trod,
By cannon peal and flashing blade,
  The victory of God.

O land beloved, ye know full well
  God's vengeance sure and strong
Turned never backward, where it fell
  It crushed the foulest wrong.

And still ye trod through clouded years
  The wanton ways of shame,
Till voice of blood and voice of tears
  Called down the avenging flame.

Well have ye learned by storm and blood
  In fierce war's fiery van,
How vain to lift for help to God
  The chains that shackle man.

Lift up your heads, O dusky race!
   Above Wrong's fading frown
Sits Justice with her patient face,
   With manhood's robe and crown!

ONLY TWO SUMMERS.

Sweetest Rosebud! it was meet
She should come when all things sweet
Had their waking—had their birth
For the glory of the earth.

So when springtime's bud and spray
Were touched with beauty by the May,—
When the early crocus' gold
Shook above the quickened mold
And the violets dewy wet
In the wayside nooks were set;—
When arbutus' breath revealed
All its blossoms though concealed
Under dead leaves old and gray
Of the summers passed away;—
With the bloom of apple-trees
And the hum of golden bees,
With the cherry clumps o'errun
With foamy blossoms in the sun,
With the sweetest music trilled
By the song-birds as they build
'Mid the branches' woven shade,
Then in angel light arrayed,
Down from Heaven's pearly gate
Strayed one day the baby Kate.

Little do we dream or know
How the lilies bloom and grow,—
How from sun and air and mold
Build they cups of pearl and gold
Neither can we know or say
How our Rosebud day by day,
Grew to beauty in the land
Silently as flowers expand,
Only this we know is true,
Never bud or blossom grew
Where the golden sunbeams fall—
She was fairer than them all.

Sweeter than the sweetest thought
Was the music that she brought.
Truly dimpled hands outreach
With more eloquence than speech.
Do not dainty finger-tips,
Rosy cheeks and rosy lips,—
Cooing tones, like mated birds,
That lack the rounded form of words,
Little pattering feet at loss
How the rill of light to cross
That the sunshine quivering o'er
Pours across the shaded floor,
Match for beauty, song and worth,
All the treasures of the earth?

Who can tell the thoughts and plans
That busied little brain and hands,
While two summers' shade and shine
Stained the tulip cups with wine?
While her thoughts grew up to reach

Utterance in prattling speech,—
Sweeter far the lisping words
Than the rippling song of birds—
Summer faded;—well-a-day,
Swift the seasons glide away.
Silently the golden days
Swam away in dreamy haze,
And the winter's rain and sleet
Crushed the dead flowers under feet.

White drifts now are piled between
Two summers' damasked robes of gre
Did she hear sweet voices call—
Voices from the jasper wall?
Did the angels wish her home,
And softly beckon her to come?

How could roses boom and grow
In an atmosphere of snow?
They that have the Master's care
Bloom in Heaven's own light and air.

UNDER THE WILLOWS.

WHERE wild-birds build in quiet dells,
    And soft, sweet airs around them stray,—
In cool glades where the twilight dwells,
    We dream the hours away.

Within these wild-wood temple halls
    Where music breathes in undertone,
How cool the noon-day shadow falls
    On mossy crag and stone.

The graceful birch with silver stem
    Is fringed with wild vines trailing o'er—
Its broad tent wears the ivied hem
    It wore in days of yore.

Its tangled clumps have thicker grown,
    And hang like sunset's ruddy flames,
Against the carved trunk's snowy zone
    And over sculptured names.

O, sweep the trailing fringe aside,—
    The letters trace through dark brown stain,
While sunshine floods with golden tide
    The fading lines again.

h! rose-red lips and laughing eyes!
    Sweet angel faces, round me stand!
Fair forms that passed beyond the skies
    From childhood's sunny land.

One wears the same thick, curly hair
    And clear, glad smile he ever wore;
And one, the fairest of the fair,
    Looks toward the peaceful shore.

One stands as in the long-lost years,
    His brow by light-airs softly fanned;—
One clasping in her childish fears,
    Her brother's sun-browned hand.

Through golden years that would not stay,
    These arches rang with youthful games,
And resting here one summer day,
    We rudely carved our names.

Adown the hillside, through the shade,
   The gleaming mill-stream winds and turns,
Tangling its vine of silver braid
   Among the drooping ferns.

Bare feet tread lightly by the shore,
   Sweet lilies wave from wet, white hands,
And childhood's voices ring once more
   Along the embroidered sands.

The waves glide on, the lilies fall
   And float far down the winding stream—
The old-time voices fainter call
   The echoes through my dream.

Ah! many years the robin's nest
   Has swung in winds that moaned with cold,
And Junes, above the dreamers' rest,
   Have tossed the daisy's gold.

Far through the vista's airy sweep,
   Beyond the dusky twilight's gloom,
The meadows in their greenness sleep
   And wave their clover blooms.

And farther where the marble stands
   Beneath the willow's drooping spray,
The sleepers wait for angel hands
   To roll the stone away.

AFTER THE WAR.

It is done!
Hell has lost and heaven has won!
Thunder it from every gun!

Let the cannon's wrathful lips
Tell of treason's dark eclipse,
Let its black throat belch and blaze
In a carnival of praise
    Loud and long:—
God is just and truth is strong!

    Ring, O bells!
On the throbbing air of spring—
Breath of bloom—your gladness fling.
Beat the warm air with your praises
Till it bursts the budding daisies,
Pearl and gold and hangs the roses
Where each patriot form reposes
'Mid the storm of shot and shell,
    Where he fell!

    Lips of prayer!
Let your praises everywhere
Ring through all the crystal air.
See! the rifted clouds withdrawn!
Lo! the hill-tops bright with dawn!
And over all the war-swept scene
Falls the light of peace serene!
Awake and praise—the storm is spent,
God's smile is in the firmament!

    Sing, O Land!
God, by his almighty hand,
Hath builded thee a temple grand!
By His pillared cloud and flame
He hath led thee out from shame—
From oppression's night of gloom,

Through the Red Sea's crimson foam!
O land redeemed, awake and sing,
    The Lord is King!

    Sing, O birds!
Warble out the sweetest words
Captive ears have ever heard.
To the weary bondman call,
Where the orange blossoms fall:—
"Hearts of anguish, brows of pain,
God's own hand hath loosed thy chain!"
Flit and sing, O birds of spring,
Well may all the heavens ring
    With the nation's jubilee!

    Columbia's free!
God be praised for liberty!
Ye who waited sad and long
In your heritage of wrong,
Chained and bleeding, lashed and torn,
Watching for the coming morn,
Clash your cymbals—broken chains!—
With Miriam sing—Jehovah reigns—
  "He hath triumphed gloriously!"

    Mountain spars!
Bear aloft o'er battle's scars
The Flag of Beauty!—Flag of Stars!
Forever glow, O web of light,
More proudly burn, ye star-fires bright,
More grandly wave, o'er land and sea,
Thou emblem of true liberty!
From dust and blood ye rise to wave
Henceforth above no bleeding slave!

DAY BY DAY.

Do we gather and glean from the golden days
   The measure of good their coming brings,
Or grovel and grope in the crooked ways,
   Unfanned by the breath of the passing wings?

For the angels pass with the shining hours,
   And sweet dews fall for the buds that yearn,
And touch with beauty the drooping flowers
   That only to heaven in waiting turn.

The sweetest of manna our hearts may find
   Each morning sown for our utmost needs;—
But groping alone in the dark, and blind,
   We may fill our hands with the rankest weeds.

Shall we trample the harvest's waving gold
   Under our feet for the sluggard's bread?
Shall we feed on its bounties manifold,
   Or hunger, and shrivel, and starve instead?

O gather no more the thistles of care,
   The briars of hate and nettles of wrath,
When beautiful roses sweeten the air
   And border with beauty our daily path.

THE NEW SUCCESSION.

The temple arches of the midnight glow
With diamond splendors o'er the hills of snow.

A bended form with wrinkled visage waits
Before the threshold of the starry gates.

The old light glows and kindles in his eyes,
While past his gaze rare visions sweep and rise.

And while he waits the soft and mellow chime
Of jangled sweetness from the bells of time

Breaks into song!—the gates of midnight swing,
And he is gone!—the young New Year is King!

TRUST.

Once more the song birds set the air athrill
   With symphonies of praise,
And buds and blossoms grow to music's trill
   In warm and sheltered ways.

How fair the earth in tender green arrayed,
   How sweet the wild notes sung,
When tufted branches weave a web of shade
   And new-made nests are swung.

How know the wild-birds when to take the wing
   From Southern grove and clime?
What voices tell the dreaming earth that spring
   Has brought the waking time?

Nay, question not, nor doubt but birds can tell
   The time to come and go,—
The earth to wake the sweet flowers in the dell,
   Doth God not always know?

THE NEW YEAR.

Rare splendor of the morning fall
   On Time's heir softly down,
Who last night in the starry hall
   Of midnight took his crown;
Alone he stood beside the bier
   And bowed his shining head
In silence o'er the crownless year
   So pallid, cold, and dead!

Light up, O dawn, his untrod way!
   O bells of gladness, ring!
Crown him with joy this happy day,
   The royalest new king!
O ring till doubt and darkness flee,
   Till shadow-flags are furled,
For over land and over sea
   The New Year rules the world!

Long live the King! A happy reign!
   A loyal realm his own!
No fields be his of gory slain,
   But peace his pillared throne:
May no plague smite his heritage,
   No secret foe beguile,
But ever on from youth to age
   May golden plenty smile!

O New Year, hailed with joy to-day,
   Through all thy kingdom's span,
Work in thy reign the blessed sway
   Of love that conquers man!
Leave room no more for feud and hate,

Nor place for cruel scorn,
Sweep hollow shams from church and state,—
Be peace and good-will born!

Speed on, O year, the time foretold,—
　By bard and minstrel sung;
Lead on the coming age of gold,
　And give its praise a tongue:
So shall dissension's voice be stilled,
　While strife and malice flee,
And earth's green hills and vales be filled
　With sweetest charity.

KING MIDAS.

Once in the golden long ago,—
　So says mythology,
The god Silenus old and gray
　Went out upon a spree,
And got as drunk the records say,
　As any man might be!

And so it chanced while in this plight,
　And reeling round one day,
Some merry clowns who crossed his path
　Made him an easy prey,
And led him thus unto their king
　To see what he would say.

King Midas saw his maudlin state
　With bitter grief and pain,
And cared for him all tenderly
　Since drink had been his bane,

Till old Silenus sober grew,
　And was himself again.

And then a royal feast was spread
　All ordered by the crown,
　　days of music, mirth, and cheer,
　Through all the goodly town,
To honor this hilarious god
　Who now had sobered down!

The banquet done, the music hushed,
　The echoes silent grown,
The generous god approached the king
　Who sat upon his throne,
And begged that he would ask of him
　Some boon for favors shown.

Now Midas was a greedy king
　As ever reigned of old—
If we believe what chroniclers
　Have plainly writ and told—
For nothing here was half so fair
　To him as yellow gold.

And so he craved of old Silene
　That all his hands should clasp,
Or even touch, might turn to gold
　Within his very grasp:—
A very foolish thing indeed
　For any king to ask!

Straightway the boon was granted him:
　Ah, happy king, you say,
To have his coffers heaped and filled
　In such a charming way—

Such countless stores of yellow gold
   And none to say him nay!

And so King Midas thought himself,
   And with his might and main
He wrought with his celestial charm
   To win him golden gain,
Till weary with his toil he paused
   With hunger's gnawing pain!

The board was spread, the outpoured wine
   Like rubies flashed and burned,
But on his lips to yellow dust
   The mellow liquid turned!
His touch transformed his very food!
   And left him starved and spurned!

And when to quench his burning thirst,
   His outstretched hands would seize
The luscious fruit, he found it grown
   In far Hesperides,
And cursed with golden food he fell
   Upon his royal knees,

And earnestly besought the gods
   That they would him behold,
While he confessed his greed and shame
   And penitently told
How daily gifts of heaven surpass
   The touch that turns to gold.

From morn till noon, from noon till night
   From dusky eve till dawn
Swept in her robes of royal state
   Across the palace lawn,

MY QUEST.

He begged the gods unceasingly
   To have the boon withdrawn.

The gods propitious heard his cry.
   And took his charm again,
And bade him bathe where Pactolus
   Rolls on to meet the main,
And lo! its borders gleamed with gold,
   And golden still remain!

And still the river winds to-day,
   Though centuries have trod
Across its shining sands of gold
   With lifted scepter rod,
And babbles of a foolish king
   And of a drunken god.

MY QUEST.

My friend with me one summer hour
   Strolled in the waning light,
But while I paused to pluck a flower,
   He passed beyond my sight.

I marveled not, the path did wind
   And turn so much; I said,
My eager steps the lost will find
   A little way ahead.

So fared I as the foot-path led
   Till long the distance grew;
Alas! his silent feet had sped
   Yet farther than I knew.

And still my eager quest is vain;
   No lisp of song or sound,
Brings healing for my growing pain,
   The lost is yet unfound!

So late he walked the busy street,
   The crowded ways of men,
I half expect 'mid those I meet
   To see him come again.

What spell can stay his willing feet?
   O summer winds far blown,
Waft back some word of comfort sweet,
   Some old familiar tone!

Somewhere he waits though foot-path turns
   And crags shut out the light:
I know the star in beauty burns
   Though it be out of sight.

So while I watch the ebbing sands
   A faith not wholly dead,
Whispers sometimes of clasping hands
   Not very far ahead.

A BATTLE RELIC.

(FORT WILLIAM HENRY.)
1757.

A MISSILE of hate from the field of death,
   Battered and bruised among the spheres
It hurtled against in the battle's breath,
   And gnawed by the rust of a hundred years

From the land it ploughed in the days of old,
   By the sylvan lake's bewitching grace,
The ploughshare turned from the mellow mold
   The crusted shot from its hiding place.

From its dreamless rest by the peaceful shore,
   From the sleep of a century lone and long,
It comes again to the light once more,
   The theme of the minstrel's humble song.

And this is the story it tells of shame,
   The murderous deeds of a savage clan,
The withering blight on a soldier's name—
   The broken faith of a perjured man.

Full softly the light of the dawning fell
   Across the lake in a rosy glow,
And lighted the rude old fortress well,
   That morn of a hundred years ago—

That morn when the winged missile flew
   To its dreamless rest from a throat of flame,
While the notes that the bugle sternly blew
   Closed the gap it made in the ranks of fame:

Ere the flush of the sunset laid its spell
   On the heights where the fair morn looked and smiled,
The fortress's banners forever fell
   And its brave lay dead in the lonely wild.

And the smoke of battle and ruin filled
   The valley of death, and the mouldering brand

Marked the ghastly scene, while the wilderness
    thrilled
  With a shudder that crept through the des-
    olate land.

———

More than a hundred years have swept,
  Across the vale where the fortress stood,
While the murderous shot in the earth has slept,
  Crusted and marred and stained with blood.

And this is the story the missile tells
  Of the sack and siege by the treacherous foe
By the beautiful lake in the mountain dells
  More than a hundred years ago!

"THE HERB CALLED HEART'S-EASE."

Nay, nay, 'tis but a legend old,
  A fable, not a truth,
Like that which led the Spaniard long
  To seek the fount of youth.

And so I said there is no land
  To-day that gives it room,
No patient star looks down upon
  Its sweet and perfect bloom.

Perchance in some far distant clime
  Its fragrance once was shed,
But now it lingers here no more,
  The plant is long since dead.

The years passed on :—my garden close,
  Which I had thought so fair,
Took seed one day from passing wings,
  Which grew to something rare.

A lowly plant at first it seemed,
  But grew from grace to grace,
Till brooding peace o'er-shadowed it,
  And rested in the place.

And strangely still its beauty grows
  And swings its bloom in air,—
No more a myth, or legend old,
  For Heart's-ease groweth there!

ON THE HILLS.

Along the hillside's tender green
  The winding footpath strays,
Still mounting toward the breezy heights
  We climbed in other days.

Across the clover fields of bloom
  The rarest odors pass,
All silently as shadows drift
  Above the waving grass.

Upon the wayside rocks I lean
  And watch the sunset glow,
So like the golden light that fell
  On us so long ago.

So fair! and yet the perfect grace
  The olden landscape wore,—

The years will never bring again,
  Nor yet my loss restore.

For while the songs of brook and bird
  Are trembling on my ear,
One sweeter strain of other days
  I can no longer hear.

Could but the same old sunset fires
  Upon the hill-tops burn,
And all the loss of vanished years
  To me again return,

Alone I need not climb the way
  All wearily and slow;—
But you are on the hills of heaven,
  And I the hills below.

TO H. W. LONGFELLOW ON HIS BIRTHDAY.

O rare sweet singer whom the nations honor,
  For whom the people pray,
How many hands are lifted up in blessing
  Above thy head to-day!

For still a pilgrim on the busy highway,
  Now sloping toward the sea,
Thou leanest to-day upon the Golden Milestone—
  Three-score and ten and three.

It is thy birthday: where thy songs have wandered
  Glad hearts will speak thy name,

And twine affection's roses with the laurel
   Of thy undying fame.

How fair thy crown! How grand thy poet mission!
   To wing with truth thy song;—
To lift the head bowed low in bitter anguish,
   To make the weary strong!

O songful gleaner in the fields of story!—
   From meadows near and far,
From starry voices softly o'er us bending,
   Thou teachest what we are.

Thy magic pen, like wand of the magician,
   Waves o'er the dark unseen,—
And lo! in love's own royal grace and beauty,
   Walks forth Evangeline.

For thy sweet song is hushed the voice of weeping
   By firesides lone and sad,
Till doubt departs and sorrow is transfigured
   To hope that maketh glad.

We joy with thee:—for even as love's evangel
   Breathes through thy mellow lay,
From loyal hearts a silent benediction
   Descends on thee to-day!

So fare thee on, adown the slope descending,
   Led by His gracious hand,
So shalt thou bear at last "Hope's tender blossoms
   Into the Silent Land."

"WATCHMAN! WHAT OF THE NIGHT?"

To-day the bugle's battle hymn
    Is ringing from its throat of gold,
And War's red lips are fiercely grim
    With mutterings of the wrongs of old;
The measured tramp of armies breaks
    The quiet hush, the peaceful calm,
The dreaming echo starts and wakes
    To hear the cannon's murderous psalm.

It rings through all the stormy din,
    Above the wrathful billow's swell,
The wild unrest of treason's sin—
    The loathed and hated spawn of hell;
Amid its solemn pause we hear
    The ragged curse of dying wrong,
And then it swells so full and clear,
    We know 'tis Freedom's deathless song!

Though millions weep, the noble slain
    Who wear their badge of glorious scars,
Who sleep and dream upon the plain
    Their loyal dreams beneath the stars;—
The battle-troubled wave of time
    To-day which rolls and cannot rest,
Shall bear through all the years sublime
    A deepening glory on its crest!

Lo! gleaming shafts of cheering light
    Flash up to heaven their golden spires,
They point to God through all the night—
    Eternal Freedom's altar fires!
And they shall burn despite the blood

In crimson storms upon them rained,
And naught can stay the arm of God
From justice to the scourged and chained!

We know the golden day will dawn,
Though night be dark, and stars be dim,
When Freedom, flooded by the morn,
Shall wake like Memnon, with a hymn:
For God is just who reigns on high,
And wrath divine, which slumbered long,
Is falling from the brightening sky
Upon the reeling hosts of wrong.

The clustering stars our banner bears
In constellated light shall glow,
Though Treason kindle direst wars
And crimson rivers stream and flow,
No star-bedimmed—no Pleiad lost!
No reign of chaos' wildest night
Shall quench one beam of peerless cost,
Or stain one spray of purest light!

God speed the day whose dawning hour
Shall flood with light the crimson rain,
And see the avenging arm of power
Sweep from Columbia every stain;—
And crush foul Treason's hydra head
'Neath Freedom's bannered stars unfurled,
And Right, and Might, and Justice wed
Through all the kingdoms of the world.

1864.

PASSING THE LIGHT.

As one who sails the blue waves of the sea,
  By wind and wave borne on across the foam,
By night oft passes where the headlands lift
  Their steady lights by which he steers for home
So we, borne on across the sea of years,
  Long tossed, but gaining on the homeland shore
While stars dip down along the fading track
  And brighter constellations rise before,
Pass once again the beacon's friendly light
  Whose genial glow lies on the waters cold,
And kindles far along the homeward track,—
  On spar and sail the storms so oft enfold;
And on we drift where tides turn never back,
  And this way lie the shining capes of gold.

FOR THE BRAVE.

  The murky clouds of war have flown,
    Our battle-flags are furled,
  The cannon's breath no more is blown
    Across the startled world.

  The stormy years of strife have fled,
    The peace which reigns to-day,
  Was won by blood of martyred dead
    Beneath the flowers of May.

  We breathe the freshened air that fills
    The summer dome of blue
  And fans with life our northern hills,
    Since they were brave and true.

For them the kindly May returns
  With generous sun and showers,
And o'er our martyred heroes yearns
  With all her soul of flowers.

We hold them brave and loyal yet,
  And twine with greener sprays,
A fresh wreath round their memories, set
  With bud and bloom of praise.

FOR A CRYSTAL WEDDING.

When Adam left the guarded gate
  To wander far and wide,
One ray of sunshine cheered his fate—
  Eve wandered by his side;
And though their weary feet did press
  The waste for many a mile,
Love planted all the wilderness,
  And made the desert smile.

O sacred bond of heavenly birth
  That makes the world so fair!—
The richest legacy to earth
  Since loss of Eden rare;—
Sweet boon to gladden high and low
  And light each clouded way,
With home's bright altar-fires which glow
  Where wedded love holds sway.

Since earth in darkness may have wheeled
  Through rayless realms of cold
Had bridal bells no gladness pealed,

Nor plighted vows been told;—
We well may clasp the angel hand
 Of Love that reaches down,
And hail the light of Eden-land
 Which comes our race to crown!—

Alas! the years, how swift they pass,
 How fleet the seasons fly!
Old Father Time with scythe and glass
 Is always jogging by;
No shady wayside cool and sweet
 Can ever lure to stay,
Or pause to rest his weary feet
 A moment by the way.

Still on and on his pathway runs
 Through lands of blight and bloom,
'Neath tropic heat of summer suns
 And frozen wastes of gloom;
With bended form and wrinkled face
 And shadowed brow of pain,
He journeys on with solemn pace
 And ne'er returns again!

We may not stay his silent flight
 Nor hope to lure him back,
Yet memory sifts her sands to-night
 Far down his beaten track;
And lighted by their golden glow
 Again the past appears,
Far winding through the vale below
 Of fair but vanished years!

We need no magic glass to see
 The valley leading down,

FOR A CRYSTAL WEDDING.

The hill-slope and the spreading tree,
   The farm-house old and brown:—
Just as it stood, to-day it stands,
   While vines are trailing low,
To shut it in from meadow lands,
   As years and years ago.

What plighted vows were whispered here!—
   What sweet romances spun!
In that divinest atmosphere
   What golden dreams begun!—
You know it all; I need not tell
   The story never old,
First learned in Eden's shady dell
   And since through ages told!

And so we joy with you to-night
   Full loyally and true,
By day your pathway glows, with light,
   By night the stars shine through;
For Love hath winged the weary feet
   And sunshine crowned the day,
While childhood's voices clear and sweet,
   Have gladdened all the way.

Dear friends whom now we greet and cheer!
   Heaven's blessing on your store,
And still through every changing year
   God speed you more and more,—
Till all the weary miles are passed
   And shadows merge in sun,
Where life's long valley ends at last
   And golden heights are won!

DECORATION DAY.

While through the loyal land to-day
    Whose peace no passion mars,
The mellow bugles ring and play,
    The old flag lifts its stars.

Above the green and grassy mounds
    Where hands are crossed in rest,
The sweetest Mayflowers' woven crowns
    Are laid on valor's breast.

The rarest blooms of sun and rain
    Are not too sweet nor fair,
To deck the silent ranks of slain
    Who sleep in glory there.

Where red war swept the wasted land
    With fever-breath of flame,
They bore the battle's lifted brand
    In freedom's sacred name.

The green earth gives them quiet room,
    And guards them far and near;
She gives her bud and leaf and bloom,
    Nor holds her gifts too dear.

And those who sleep where none may know,
    Unmarked by stone or name,—
Who heed not how the seasons go—
    The voice of praise or blame,

Kind nature keeps with tender care,
    The stars watch from above,
And May-time sets her glad smile there
    With all its wealth of love.

Above their dreams the grasses lean
    Through all the summer days,
To keep their loyal memories green
    With tenderest meed of praise.

And where they lie in all the land,
    On plain, or mountain's crest,
Sweet May has spread with lavish hand
    Her flowers above their rest.

A NEW YEAR'S GREETING.

To J. G. W.

FROM southern slopes still clad in sober brown,
Where briefer winter breathes in milder gales
Than those that sweep thy own New England vales
And hills of white beneath a snowy crown,
I send thee greeting: though the skies may frown
And bitter chill hold all the land in thrall,
One heart, in love, would blessing on thee call;—
God send on thee his peace and quiet down.
Thrice Happy New Year! O my friend, to thee!
Each golden hour from ill bear sweet release,
May sunshine bid each dusky shadow flee,
And o'er thee shine the blessed stars of peace.
God crown thee well and make thy journey long,
Whose four-score years have gladdened earth with
    song.

TO A DEAD POET.

O FRIEND who sang of "Summer Dreams,"
   How hushed thy mellow lay,
How dark the world without thee seems.
   Where strayest thou to-day?

We know not where thy footsteps are,
   But in thy manhood's prime,
We know that thou hast wandered far
   Beyond the gates of time.

So far, and yet no word of thine,
   Nor laurel freshly won,
Breathed faintest hint, or secret sign,
   That half thy work was done!

Was that a prophecy inwrought
   Upon thy pictured page,
Where glows the poet's golden thought
   With wisdom of the sage?

Three vases there hold precious hoard;
   In two the wealth is told,
And from the broken crystal poured,
   Is seen the ruddy gold.

But one, unbroken, still is sealed,
   And holds its treasure fast,
Till on the glowing page revealed,
   Behold the third, and last!

And didst thou know, so young and strong,
   When life with love was sweet,
That breaking this fair vase of song
   Would make thy task complete?

It may be thus: we may not know
    What new sense nearness brings,
Since some have felt the daisies grow,
    And heard the noise of wings!

Rest on, O friend! the guerdon won,
    And sweet thy rest shall be;
Dream on, thy work is nobly done,
    And love shall follow thee.

Thy goal was not this shadow-land,
    But far beyond the blue,
And thou hast reached the golden strand,
    And all thy dreams are true!

DICKENS IN WESTMINSTER ABBEY.

Amid the silent throng,
Immortal grown in song,
We trace his carven name,
So dear to deathless fame.
Praise cannot flatter him
Beyond the border din,
Though love's sweet flowers may shed
Their fragrance round him dead,
Within the solemn gloom
That watches o'er his tomb.

Since where he lived and wrought
They bless him for his thought,
Not less to-day, may we
Revere his memory.
Though dead his influence thrills
O'er all the tented hills — :

Where'er his native tongue
In melody has rung,
On every land and shore
His fame lives evermore!

Who by his magic power
Lighted the gloomy hour,
And with his wizard pen
Made glad the hearts of men
On whom no ray was shed
From starlight overhead;—
Who for the lowliest lot
Touched the dark leprous spot
Of want and woe and sin,
And let the sunshine in;—
Who wrought as best he could
To lure all men to good,
And so by loyal ways
From all hearts gathered praise—
Him can no people claim,
For world-wide is his fame.

Proud England laid him down,
Made royal by no crown
Save that which genius brings
Amid her queens and kings.
With folded hands at rest
Upon his manly breast—
The minster gloom his pall,
The kingliest king of all!

There in the Abbey old
Where twilights soft enfold
Beneath their dusky wings

The garnered dust of kings
We muse amid the gloom
Beside his loyal tomb,
'Neath fretted arch and wave—
His grand cathedral grave.

Around him here and there
In the great fane of prayer
Are kings in days of old
Under the marbles cold;—
Queens who reigned and died,
Now lying side by side;—
Queen Bess of royal fame,
And Mary of Scottish name,
Long lines of princely sway,
Whose thrones have passed away,—
Almost their names unknown
Except for carven stone;
Soldiers whose brows austere
Have gloomed a hemisphere;
The hero of peace so grand
Brought home from Afric's land;
Statesmen whose words are still
Nerving the heart and will;
Poets whose songs sublime
Will ring through coming time;
And him who saw afar
Beyond the utmost star
The law which all outruns,
Threading the stars and suns!
Such is the silent throng
Waiting around him long.

But when the waning light,
Through Chancel's window dight
With storied pilgrim train
Of old romance again,
Touches with fading glow
Statue and tomb below,
While dusky twilight waits
Before the starry gates
In beauty wide unfold,
What visions are unrolled!

Perchance 'twill only seem
As but an idle dream:
But when the organ's tone
Trembles through every stone,
And rolls its swelling wave
Through chapel, crypt, and nave,
The children of his brain
Throng round him there again,
And through the mystic glow
Pass forms that you may know!
Yonder with shining face
And form of manly grace,
A portly form draws near,
Whom sages nod to hear!
And one whose hopeful smile
Beams sweetly all the while,
Still trusting more and more
For greater good in store.
Another passes near
Through the dusky atmosphere,
His hungry youth is o'er,
He pleadeth not for more,

But in his manhood's pride,
With beauty by his side,
He seemeth satisfied.

Hard-hearted, grim and old
Bends Scrooge above his gold,
While ghastly, pale and shy,
Old Marley's ghost flits by!
Not least amid them all
Is Dombey's little Paul;
So fair, yet full of pain,
Borne on amid the train,
He hears the waves at play
Still wondering what they say.

Now through the shadows dim
Stalks Squeers, the master grim,—
Type of the soulless greed
That fattens on childhood's need,—
While Fagin with thievish leer,
And fiendish Quilp appear.

There pillowed on her bed,
Passes a shiny head,
As though some sunny sheen
Had softly slid between
The shadows, making clear
The dusky atmosphere;
They stand about her there
As tranced in solemn prayer,
And when the shadow falls
Darker on Abbey walls,
With heart-ache none can tell
They weep for Little Nell.

The shadows deepen where
Waves Little Dorrit's hair;
Round Barnaby's wild joy,
And Dot's entrancing boy;
Round Nickleby, the tried,
And Copperfield beside,
And hosts I cannot name,
All born to deathless fame.

Moonrise is in the sky;—
The phantoms fade and fly,
As stars are lost in light
They vanish out of sight;
And drawing near his grave
In the great temple's nave,
My withered buds of praise
I lay beside the bays
Which faithful love has thrown
Upon his sculptured stone,
And leave amid the gloom
The dead magician's tomb.

THE DYING YEAR.

"The King is dead!—
Long live the King!"

The year's last sunset burning low
  Has faded from the sky,
And all the hill-tops white with snow
  Have blushed to see it die.

Where first he stood in kingly might
  To take his shining crown,

The year will pause awhile to-night
   To lay his sceptre down.

And in the lonely midnight hall—
   His royal splendors fled—
Old winter's white-frilled robe will fall
   To hide his crownless head.

The stars will lend their fitful gleam
   To gild the midnight snows,
So softly folded o'er his dream
   In sleep's sublime repose.

So passes all his glorious prime
   As endless years have done,
Since first the morning hills of time
   Grew golden in the sun.

And while we fondly linger near,
   The final dream unsought,
We hold the Old Year's memory dear
   For all the good he wrought.

So kindly was his gentle sway,
   So glad his golden reign,
We linger by his closing day
   And wish him crowned again.

Lo! how through all the waiting land
   Beneath his lifted crown,
His train went forth—in beauty grand
   To scatter largess down!

On rich and poor alike has laid
   The bounty he has won,

While once again the world has made
    The circuit of the sun.

He called the earth from slumbers deep,
    He broke her frozen dream,
And warmed the sluggish pulse of sleep
    With springtime's sunny gleam :

Till all the tides of life grew strong
    Through nature's hidden ways,—
Till wind and wave and bird and song
    Were glad with summer's praise.

From songful rain and golden sheen
    When winter storms were furled,
He wrought the meadow's woven green,
    The harvests of the world.

The luscious fruits of autumn-time
    Were scattered in his train,
And where he passed in every clime
    Were garners heaped with grain.

If ever o'er his peaceful path
    The baleful fires have spread
Of lurid passion's kindled wrath,
    Of battle's stormy tread ; —

If in some vine-wreathed land afar
    Where summer laughed and leaned
Beneath the deadly plague's red star,
    The silent Reaper gleaned ;

If 'neath the sunshine's gracious smile
    Within the Old Year's reign,

Want's ghastly presence stood awhile
   And cast its spell of pain;

His breath across the azure bay—
   The shoreless sea of blue,
Far swept the murky clouds away
   And let the sunbeams through.

And over wave and over wood
   He poured the mellow shine,
That stayed the reaper where he stood
   Amid the hills of vine.

From stores of plenty's golden grain
   His bounty ripened well,
He stilled the cry of hunger's pain
   Where blight and famine fell.

And every land beneath the sun
   Has felt his genial sway,
His gracious ministries have run
   World-wide their shining way.

And when the starry line drew near
   No sandalled foot hath trod,
He brought the kindly Christmas cheer,
   The gracious gift of God.

When peace on earth, good-will below,
   On wings of song uprose,
He paused above the hills of snow
   As waiting for its close.

Awhile beneath the patient blaze
   Of starry midnight's spell,

He turned below his longing gaze
   On lands he loved so well.

But when the solemn chimes were told
   Above his royal head,
Low drooped his sceptre's frosted gold—
   The crownless king was dead!

Alas! alas! the gray Old Year!
   This wreath of song we bring
To lay upon his white-robed bier;—
   Then cry—"Long live the King!"

LINES

Read on the Tenth Anniversary of St. John's Literary Association, Sept. 17, 1885, Concord, Pa.

ALAS, for me! no help is mine,
   I build my tower alone;
Not one of all the singing nine
   Will lift a hand, or stone.

How sweetly some are born to shine
   Without a thought or care;
While some in sorrow must repine,
   Or borrow what they wear.

The dandelion's disc of gold
   When all its race is run,
Is but a nodding gray-beard old—
   A seed-globe in the sun!

The ragged thistle, brave and gay,
   Keeps all its sabres keen—

When frailer blooms are passed away,
   Its armor still is green.

The brightest colors quickly fade,
   All fashions have their day;
The dude will mildew in the shade,
   When sober sense will stay.

What limitations hedge us round!
   But set the pinion free,
How might we scale the closing bound!—
   What sages might we be!

The soaring thought would rise and grow—
   Its wings unfurl in air;—
The mind immortal grasp and know
   The how and why and where!

Canst tell how white-rimmed daisies grow?
   Where drift the clouds away?
Why all the leaves do whisper so
   Or what the wild waves say?

In vain, in vain, we question so;
   The anxious thought returns;—
But oh, to scale this height and know—
   How hope aspires and burns!

So runs our dream—we sleep and wake—
   Nor know the how or why
Of half the common things that break
   Upon our longing eye!

Still hangs our being's pictured scroll—
   So pass the shadows by,

While golden years of life unroll
   Beneath a changeful sky.

A wondrous web of woven days,
   All crossed by changeful bars
Of rising morns, and noontide blaze—
   Of setting suns and stars.

Whereon a glowing picture stands,
   A strange design appears,
All blindly wrought by careless hands
   Through light or clouded years.

A greening leaf—a bud full blown—
   A blotch of autumn's gold—
So soon the perfect flower is grown,
   So soon its life is told!

Behold the lilies, how they grow!
   Rare green and gold their crown,
Or whiter than the drifted snow,
   They drop their petals down.

Their glory passes quickly by,
   So soon their robes are lost!
While hazels bloom 'neath winter's sky
   Unmindful of the frost.

So in the meadow's pictured lin
   And in the gardens crowned,
In blooms that neither toil nor spin
   Our changing state is found.

Above the fair green-bladed hills
   Our footsteps tread to-day,

LINES.

What light the bended heaven fills!—
    What shadows flee away!

The rugged path with song is rife
    'Neath fortune's favored smile,
While birthdays build the shrines of life
    Where each may rest awhile.

The way is long—so pause we here,
    Though heaven be clear or wild,
We come from far—we come from near,
    With greetings for our child!

Ten years ago, 'mid autumn days,
    Whose glory crowned the earth—
Amid the Indian summer's haze
    Our nurseling had her birth.

This is her birthday!—only ten!—
    A goodly child and strong;
What grace through all the walks of men
    She bears amid the throng!

If half a score of years unfold
    Such matchless beauty rare,
When other added years are told
    What will the measure bear?

All hail St. John's!—the name we tell
    Still lingers on the tongue,
To-night for her our praises swell,
    And birthday bells are rung!

GLADSTONE.

Brave chieftain thou in battle's stormy van!
    Thy snowy hair is more than regal crown—
    White badge of triumph over error's frown,
Through toilful years where thou hast wrought for
    man!
Opposed by greed and blinded faction's clan
    Bravely thy words the burning wrong assail!
    Take heart—hope on! The right shall yet
    prevail!—
Truth lives forever!—wrong the briefest span.
    Thou canst not fail!—the work so well begun,
    The passing years can never long delay;
Thine be the triumph when the strife is done,
    When hate shall yield to love and pass away.
Proud England then, forgetful of her shame,
Shall crown her son and keep his deathless fame!
1886.

TO A NONAGENARIAN.

    Thy pilgrim feet have journeyed far
        Beyond the measured span—
    The three-score years and ten that bar
        The weary life of man.

    As one upon some mountain's crown
        Stands in the golden gleam,
    Of broad horizons bending down,
        Aglow with sunset's dream,—

So standest thou upon the height
   Whose glory now appears,
Transfigured in the mellow light
   Of ninety golden years!

A mount of vision! far and wide
   The goodly landscape lies,
Far reaching to the morning tide
   Beneath the glowing skies.

While fair the winding valleys sleep
   In deep repose below,
May all the forward slope still keep
   The sunset's rosy glow!

So shall the light of eventide
   Fall round you where you stand,
Till all the starry gates swing wide
   To show the Morning Land!

FOR A SILVER WEDDING,

DEAR friends from out the blinding storm
   Of winter's sullen sway,
From hearts with old-time memories warm,
   We send you cheer to-day.

A Happy New Year! well you know
   What joy the greeting bears—
How all the past stands out aglow
   Above its vanished cares.

Well may you turn and backward gaze
   O'er paths your feet have trod—

O'er sunward slopes and shaded ways,
   Beneath the smile of God.

From toil-worn heights of glowing noon
   How short the way appears,
Where two have trod with sandal-shoon
   The half of fifty years!

So take your wayside rest to-day,
   O friends, and still be strong:—
God's peace make fair your future way,
   And ever glad with song.

As down the winding slope you turn
   Where autumn's sun-tints gleam,
May all the kindly lights that burn
   Show true your fairest dream!

Fly on, O wedded days of gold,
   As shadows sweep the lawn:—
God grant when all the years are told,
   You hear the bells of dawn!

MORNING.

Faintly stars are gleaming
   On the brow of day,
Softly shadows stealing
   From the world away;
Rosy light of morning
   Gilds the clouds unfurled
Waving like a banner
   O'er the waking world.

Golden sunbeams falling
   Over hill and plain,
Wreathing forms of beauty
   Float to heaven again;
Pearly dew-drops sleeping,
   'Mid the blushing flowers,
Flashing gems of beauty,
   Gleaming from the bowers.

weetly bird-notes chiming,
   With the gushing streams,
Rippling through the shadows,
   Floating, murmuring dreams;
Loftly floats the music
   On the balmy air—
Morning, glorious morning,
   Smiling everywhere!

ABSENCE.

O SUMMER days, why linger so?
Why idly o'er the meadows go?
When Love was here and hand in hand
We walked together through the land,
You sped so swiftly on your way
We sued to have you pause and stay.

O wouldst thou then the secret know,
Why thus so dreamily we go?
Why by the breath of roses fanned
We linger idly o'er the land?—
Ah! fleet wings weary in their flight
Always when Love is out of sight!

Then hasten Love and homeward flee
To arms that wait to welcome thee!
Nor flight of days, or swift or slow,
Shall keep us from the joys we know,
When side by side and hand in hand
We walk again the summer land.

A SUMMER MADRIGAL.

I'M wandering by the brookside
  With Mary Ann to-day,
The while I fan my classic brow
  And brush the flies away,
And I shall linger here full long
  If Mary Ann will stay!

The singing brook runs on and on
  As in a quiet dream,
And all the meadow hills around
  Are mirrored in the stream—
The very lilies in the brook
  Give back a fairer gleam!

The shadows lie so sweet and cool,
  The grove with rapture thrills,
The fishes seek the reedy pools
  To cool their crimson gills,
While singing ducks glide down the stream
  And liquidate their bills!

The August sun is at its best,
  The pigeons flit and coo,
Pet here along the brookside
  The tempered air will do—

Though doubtless hot for three, or more,
   It's cool enough for two!

We heed no more the heated term
   Though mercury rise like leaven,
Or soar upon its seething wing
   Way over ninety-seven—
Have we not, 'mid the shadows here,
   Almost a taste of heaven?

What vistas ope—what scenes appear?
   What airy rainbows span
Our winding path with not a breath
   To mar the dream, or ban—
I think it most exquisite here—
   And so does Mary Ann!

THE AGE OF GOLD.

In every land—in every favored clime,
All down the ages since the birth of time,
Each puny king has sought to set his name
High over all upon the lists of fame,
And thrones and kingdoms tottering to their fall
Have deemed their age the wisest, best of all.

So through all lands where war's red course has run
And conquest spread its borders 'neath the sun,
Where might has ruled as with an iron sway,
While right, defenseless, could but weep and pray,
The bards have sung, and sages wise have told
The shining splendors of the Age of Gold.

So classic Greece amid the purple seas
Sang in her time the age of Pericles.

When shone the sun on such a land as this,
So grandly crowned with her Acropolis?
There proudly sprang the Parthenon sublime—
The marble wonder of the latest time—
Whose sculptured friezes as a written scroll
Her deeds of glory to the world unroll.
Rare splendors live on history's glowing page
To mark the era of her golden age,
While fane and temple, rent and crumbled down,
Declare the glory of her old renown.

The later bards have sung in measured rhyme
The grander glories of the Roman time,
When wise Augustus ruled with golden sway,
And Rome was changed to marble from its clay.
Then sprang and grew those grand, heroic lays,
Which from the ages take their meed of praise;
Then Tully's thunders in the senate hurled,
Shook thrones and kingdoms and the Roman world;
Her name and fame the conquering legions bore
In royal triumph to the farthest shore,
And tribute brought from olden lands and new
Proclaimed how far the Roman eagle flew.

Her glory faded—still her bards remain
And live immortal in the epic's strain;
And Cæsar's palace even in decay
But shadows faintly that imperial day,
Whose brightness faded with its slow decline,
While dust is heaped on Cæsar's royal line!

Fair Albion throned amid the stormy roar
Of northern seas that beat her rocky shore,
Full proudly gloried in the golden sheen

That centred round her stately, virgin queen ;—
An age of learning worthily enrolled
As royal England's boasted age of gold,

When valiant Sidney told in golden phrase
The simple story of Arcadian days,
And dreaming Spenser saw with vision keen
The charming guest of beauty's Fairy Queen ;—
When Shakespeare reared the drama's mighty fame
And peopled it from his prolific brain,—
And later, Milton sang, in strains sublime,
The grandest epic known to any time ;—
Search through the ages—still it will be found—
No brighter era has her annals crowned.

And so all lands reveal on history's page
Some favored time they call the golden age,—
Some shining era glowing with renown,
Whose light and beauty are the nation's crown.
Yet grander far than all the ages flown
The grand to-day—the age we call our own
How far surpassing any ancient dream
The magic wonders of the age of steam !
The age that tames the lightning's fiery will
And zones the world with thought's electric thrill !
How grander yet than deed of olden fame
The spoken word borne on the wing of flame !
And far transcending all the ages done,
The electric light, resplendent as the sun !

If any age from time's first morning down
Might claim to wear the brightest, starriest crown,
Or highest write its most resplendent name
In curves of light on beaded roll of fame,

That age is passing in its splendor now—
We claim the crown for fair Columbia's brow!
For resting now from battle's wrathful jars,
She wears in peace her constellated stars.

But not for her the golden age we claim—
A grander light shall gild, at last, her name,
To finer grace her changing beauty grow,
In purer light her living annals glow.
The mighty past, the present age sublime,
Are but the prelude to a grander time,
Whose dawning splendors yet will surely rise
To gladden earth and fill the waiting skies.

And when its morn shall grow to noon-tide ray,
The Prince of Peace shall bear divinest sway;—
Then through all lands as bards have sung and told,
Shall come at last the one true Age of Gold!

All hail the day whose faintest dawn appears
To brown the cloudless glory of the years,
When man shall rise forevermore unbound,
Nor serf, nor slave, in any land be found;
When Circe's cup, where seeming jewels shine,
Shall tempt no more to grovel with the swine;
When wrong shall die, and war forever cease,
And earth shall know the golden reign of peace

www.ingramcontent.com/pod-product-compliance
Lightning Source LLC
Chambersburg PA
CBHW030316170426
43202CB00009B/1022